Addisford, North Devon

8

GOOD HOME COOKING

GOOD
HOME
COOKING

CAROLINE
CONRAN

Conran Octopus

INTRODUCTION

I decided to write this book to try to recapture the flavour of British cooking as I remember it and as I imagine it was in the days when it really existed. It is astonishing how fast it seems to be disappearing. Where are the bronzed hotpots, the mahogany-coloured oxtail stews, the golden apple pies and the melting greengage crumbles of memory? They are almost impossible to find today, either in people's homes or in restaurants.

Yet in the lovely countryside of Britain, people have always eaten good food. Down the deep green twisting lanes lie villages, farms and cottages where until recently vegetable gardens, orchards, cows, pigs, sheep and poultry were the main sources of food, and therefore of life. Everything was grown and reared locally, everybody enjoyed the fruits of their own or their neighbours' labours: they produced what they ate, made their own cheese, pickles and jam and devised recipes to make the most of all the produce.

It was quite hard work; a lot of preserving was necessary to keep things over the winter and to dispose of gluts of milk, apples and eggs. Country housewives often had to do their own baking, distil and concoct tinctures, perfumes and medicines and even brew their own beer in many parts of the country. Most households took a great pride in all this industry, and many women kept manuscript recipe books in which they recorded their favourite dishes. Often these books are written in several different, wonderfully elaborate hands that change as the book passed from one generation to another.

I have two of these, dating from the eighteenth century, and they are simply extraordinary. The huge quantities that people used to make is a surprise: families, or households, were very large in the eighteenth and nineteenth centuries with a lot of mouths to feed. Both books describe cheese-making, brewing and cider-making, and there are dozens of recipes for home-made wine using rhubarb, dandelions, cowslips, elderflowers — almost anything that can be gathered in quantity from the garden and hedgerow; and there are so many recipes for cakes and buns and little cheesecakes that one realises that tea was a major meal.

These manuscripts also contain sweets, remedies for palsy, toothache and ague, useful tips for cleaning horsehair sofas or white kid gloves and even recipes for curing chickens of their ailments. In fact the housewives in those days had to be very self-sufficient indeed.

People did not often eat in restaurants in the country until the twentieth century, unless they were on a journey when it was inns and post houses that provided the food. These 'hostelries' or 'hotels' often became famous for certain recipes, which were carried away by travellers and took root in other parts of the country. My recipe for pigeons with cabbage originated at the Red Lion Hotel in Fareham and found its way into an interesting cookery book called *Good Things in England*, written by Florence White and published in 1932.

The famous Stilton cheese seems to have started its official life as a manuscript recipe called 'Lady Beaumont's Cheese'. It was borrowed in 1720 by

GOOD HOME COOKING

CAROLINE CONRAN

Conran Octopus

Many and most heartfelt thanks to
Jane and Alan Davidson for their tremendous kindness
over the matter of libraries and the retrieval of books,
and to Jenny Alston for her energy and efforts,
to Caroline Hobhouse for her good advice
and research and to Gill Edden and
Sarah Bevan for their hard work
and encouragement.
C.C.

All the photographs in this book, with the exception of that
on page 118, were taken during the last ten years.

First published in 1985 by
Conran Octopus Limited
28–32 Shelton Street
London WC2 9PH

Edited by Gill Edden

ISBN 1 85029 014 8
Typeset by Hourds Typographica
Printed and bound by Graficromo SA, Spain

Contents

INTRODUCTION

I decided to write this book to try to recapture the flavour of British cooking as I remember it and as I imagine it was in the days when it really existed. It is astonishing how fast it seems to be disappearing. Where are the bronzed hotpots, the mahogany-coloured oxtail stews, the golden apple pies and the melting greengage crumbles of memory? They are almost impossible to find today, either in people's homes or in restaurants.

Yet in the lovely countryside of Britain, people have always eaten good food. Down the deep green twisting lanes lie villages, farms and cottages where until recently vegetable gardens, orchards, cows, pigs, sheep and poultry were the main sources of food, and therefore of life. Everything was grown and reared locally, everybody enjoyed the fruits of their own or their neighbours' labours: they produced what they ate, made their own cheese, pickles and jam and devised recipes to make the most of all the produce.

It was quite hard work; a lot of preserving was necessary to keep things over the winter and to dispose of gluts of milk, apples and eggs. Country housewives often had to do their own baking, distil and concoct tinctures, perfumes and medicines and even brew their own beer in many parts of the country. Most households took a great pride in all this industry, and many women kept manuscript recipe books in which they recorded their favourite dishes. Often these books are written in several different, wonderfully elaborate hands that change as the book passed from one generation to another.

I have two of these, dating from the eighteenth century, and they are simply extraordinary. The huge quantities that people used to make is a surprise: families, or households, were very large in the eighteenth and nineteenth centuries with a lot of mouths to feed. Both books describe cheese-making, brewing and cider-making, and there are dozens of recipes for home-made wine using rhubarb, dandelions, cowslips, elderflowers — almost anything that can be gathered in quantity from the garden and hedgerow; and there are so many recipes for cakes and buns and little cheesecakes that one realises that tea was a major meal.

These manuscripts also contain sweets, remedies for palsy, toothache and ague, useful tips for cleaning horsehair sofas or white kid gloves and even recipes for curing chickens of their ailments. In fact the housewives in those days had to be very self-sufficient indeed.

People did not often eat in restaurants in the country until the twentieth century, unless they were on a journey when it was inns and post houses that provided the food. These 'hostelries' or 'hotels' often became famous for certain recipes, which were carried away by travellers and took root in other parts of the country. My recipe for pigeons with cabbage originated at the Red Lion Hotel in Fareham and found its way into an interesting cookery book called *Good Things in England*, written by Florence White and published in 1932.

The famous Stilton cheese seems to have started its official life as a manuscript recipe called 'Lady Beaumont's Cheese'. It was borrowed in 1720 by

Elizabeth Scarbrow who worked as a housekeeper at Quenby Hall outside Leicester. It became known locally as Quenby cheese, and was soon being sold to the Bell Inn at Stilton in Huntingdonshire, some thirty miles away. The Bell became famous for its Stilton cheese — which was never, in fact, made in Stilton.

While recipes and certain foods travelled about the country, cooking was still heavily dependent on local produce. It was this that gave it its stability — housewives cooked and made the most of what they could get. Today Britain is so well supplied with frozen food and imported fruit and vegetables that anyone can cook more or less anything they like, from chow mein to salade niçoise, and the continuity of traditional dishes has been broken. The recipes in this book are for dishes that reflect that earlier continuity and come from a time when British home cooking was dependably, reassuringly, itself, open to some outside influences but slow to change.

I like these dishes because they have, over the centuries, developed rich, perfectly balanced combinations of flavour. They are mostly the kind of simple and honest foods that people can prepare at home, without fuss. I have included some dishes from cottages and farms, and others that originate in the larger country houses where entertaining was the great pastime and huge house parties, often going on for weeks, put the kitchens into a turmoil. Many of the recipes are old, but all are good; and where I feel that an innovation is actually an improvement, I have felt free to use it, as this is the way the best recipes have evolved. In this spirit is the recipe for rich salad dressing (page 147), made with avocado.

Methods of cooking as well as the ingredients available have changed in the twentieth century. To realise how lucky we are and how easy cooking is now, one has to know what it was like before. Take, for example, making tea. William Cobbett in his *Cottage Economy* of 1821 denounces tea drinking as wicked and wasteful. He says, 'It is impossible to make a fire, boil water, make the tea, drink it, wash up the things, sweep up the fireplace, and put all to rights again in a less space of time, upon an average than two hours . . .'. He does tend to exaggerate, but even so! Kitchens today are very different places to the ones where many of the recipes in this book originated.

In a cottage the kitchen was often the one and only room downstairs, and could be quite neat and cheerful; but in larger houses they were very often gloomy old places, half underground, with many other rooms or offices leading off them — larders, dairies, lamp rooms, boiler rooms, flower rooms, still rooms and woodsheds all had to be close at hand. Cooking over a fireplace with an open hearth was a method of cooking still common in many cottages at the beginning of this century. It meant that roasting and grilling were done over fiercely glowing wood with much use of bellows to keep the fire bright, and much turning of the spit (sometimes just a piece of twisted string suspended from the mantelpiece) to rotate the meat. Until ranges were brought in, braising was done by burying a black iron pot or salt-glazed jar containing the meat or poultry in the slow embers of a glowing fire, or by placing it in a bread oven built at the side of the main fireplace. Boiling, stewing and soup-making all took place in a big cauldron suspended on a chain over the fire.

Many kitchens did not have running water and so all water for cooking, washing and laundry had to be fetched from the village pumps, while the fuel was wood, sawn up and chopped by hand. With kitchens as basic as that, even in quite large houses, it amazes me that recipes became as complicated and interesting as they did. (To be good, a recipe does not, of course, have to be complex: Irish stew (page 70), with only three basic ingredients, has the most appetising and subtle flavour if properly made.)

But nowadays we can tackle anything. With our well designed kitchens with taps and electric kettles, liquidisers and food processors, automatic ovens, hobs, deep-fryers and grills, non-stick milk pans, stainless steel knives and saucepans and dishwashers, all these old recipes should be no trouble to make well. So why are we beginning to give up home cooking, just at the moment when it has become really easy? A recent survey, by Taylor Nelson Associates and published in *The Times*, 11 April 1985, shows that 'traditional foodstuffs are on the decline, "snacking" is on the rise as the breakdown in formal meals continues — instead of families eating together, more and more, one person is having a bite on the run.'

To those people who still like to sit down to a proper family meal and serve their own good home cooking, this book is dedicated.

Addisford, North Devon

SOUPS, STARTERS AND SAVOURIES

One of the great discoveries of our family as soup-eaters is a faulty peppermill that grinds very coarse black pepper; we have one that practically only cuts the peppercorns in half. A generous grinding of this on the top of any home-made soup — especially if it is a pale cream colour and has a little marbling of cream floating on the surface — makes all the difference.

I also like croûtons with any velvety soup, and I like fresh chives or chervil, or even chopped dill, coriander or mint, rather than the more predictable parsley for delicate soups. For hefty soups, such as leek and bacon, parsley is best, and the eye-watering black pepper essential. These soups make a complete lunch with thickly cut and spread wholemeal bread and a piece of Cheddar cheese.

The other things in this chapter are all alternatives to soup — they are typical of the rather elegant, light, beautiful food that the English regard as a proper introduction to a meal. They also make excellent snacks for supper or a quick lunch.

Watercress Soup

This is many people's favourite soup; a handful of spinach is a delicious addition.

Serves 4

2 bunches of watercress

8 oz (225 g) onions

6 oz (175 g) potatoes (mealy type)

½ stick of celery

1½ oz (40 g) butter

¼ pint (150 ml) dry white wine

1¼ pints (700 ml) best home-made chicken stock

¼ pint (150 ml) double cream

salt and pepper

Pick all the best bits from the tops of the watercress and keep them to one side.

Wash the stalks thoroughly and pick out any yellow or dead leaves. Peel and chop the onions and potatoes. Chop the celery. Melt the butter in a fairly large pan and soften the onions and celery for several minutes over a low heat, without browning. Add the potatoes and the white wine, let it bubble up and then add the chicken stock. Cook for 10 minutes, add the watercress stalks and cook for a further 20 minutes until everything is very tender.

Allow to cool a little and reduce to a fine purée in a liquidiser or food processor. Sieve and return the soup to the pan.

Chop the remaining sprigs of watercress fairly coarsely and add them to the soup. Cook for a few minutes then add the cream. Taste for seasoning and heat through.

TO SERVE
Serve plain or with either a small knob of butter or a spoonful of whipped cream in each bowl, and a quantity of very coarsely ground black pepper on top of that.

Leek and Bacon Soup

*'Now leeks are in season, for pottage full good,
And spareth the milch-cow and purgeth the blood,
These having with peason, for pottage in Lent,
Thou sparest both oatmeal, and bread to be spent.'*
Thomas Tusser HIS GOOD POINTS OF HUSBANDRY 1557

Leeks and bacon are always good together — this soup is enough for a complete lunch with brown bread and butter, thickly cut and thickly spread.

Serves 6

2 or 3 leeks

1 onion

2 potatoes (8 oz/225 g altogether)

2–3 rashers of your favourite bacon

1½ oz (40 g) butter

1½ oz (40 g) flour

2 pints (1.1 litres) home-made chicken stock

½ pint (300 ml) milk

salt and freshly ground pepper

1–2 tbsp cream

chopped parsley

Cut the leeks in half lengthways and wash them well between the leaves. Cut crossways into ½ inch (1 cm) slices. Chop the onion and cut the potatoes into cubes. Cut the bacon into ½ inch (1 cm) pieces.

Put the leeks and onion into a large pan with the bacon and butter and soften gently, without browning, for 5 minutes. Add the potatoes and stir them round, then add the flour. When it is well mixed in, add ½ pint (300 ml) stock and stir until smooth and thick. Then add the remaining stock, bring to the boil and simmer for 20 minutes.

Taste for seasoning, add the milk and, if you find the soup too thin, sieve some of it through a mouli-légumes, or purée it in a liquidiser or food processor. Return the purée to the soup.

To serve, heat through at the last minute, then add a little cream and some chopped parsley.

Lettuce Soup with Cream and Egg Yolks

Serves 6

2 lettuces — any firm type

1 onion or 2–3 shallots

1 oz (25 g) butter

1¾ pints (1 litre) best home-made chicken stock

1 glass dry white wine

bunch of celery tops, chervil, parsley, green (spring) onion tops (keep some fresh to scatter on top of soup)

2–3 egg yolks

salt and freshly ground pepper

squeeze of lemon juice to taste

¼ pint (150 ml) double cream

Slice up the lettuces, keeping back two or three of the pale leaves from the heart. Chop the onions or shallots and soften them in the butter in a large pan, without browning.

Wilt the lettuces down with the onions, then add the chicken stock, wine and bunch of herbs and simmer until everything is tender, about 15–20 minutes. Remove the bunch of herbs. Purée the soup in a liquidiser or food processor and strain back into the cleaned saucepan.

Beat the egg yolks in a bowl and add a ladleful of the hot — not boiling — soup. Whisk together well, then transfer back to the pan. Taste for seasoning and add a little lemon juice if you like. Whip the cream to a soft light foam.

TO SERVE

Heat the soup gently without boiling, stirring all the time. Stir in the whipped cream and serve scattered with very thin julienne strips of lettuce leaves and chopped spring onion tops.

In the summer the soup can be garnished with a few blue borage flowers and chives.

The milking parlour, Petrockstowe, North Devon

Summer Garden Vegetable Soup with Herbs

'The art of preparing good, wholesome palatable soups, without great expense, which is so well understood in France, and in other countries where they form part of the daily food of all classes of the people, has hitherto been very much neglected in England; yet it really presents no difficulties which a little practice, and the most common degree of care, will not readily overcome.'
Eliza Acton MODERN COOKERY FOR PRIVATE FAMILIES 1845

This soup really does present no difficulties. You can include whatever green garden vegetables you like — green beans, silver onions and asparagus would be delicious. Cook the coarse things first and then add the delicate ones.

Serves 6

3 onions

½ small new turnip (optional)

2 small leeks

2 shallots

3–4 new potatoes

1 stick of celery

2½ pints (1.4 litres) best home-made chicken stock

handful of spinach

1 bunch of watercress

1 lettuce

4 oz (100 g) shelled green peas

4 oz (100 g) shelled broad beans

salt and freshly ground pepper

few tbsp cream

1 tbsp finely chopped mixed chives, tarragon and parsley

Wash and peel the onions, turnip, leeks, shallots and new potatoes. Cut them and the celery into pieces and cook them in the stock for 15 minutes.

Meanwhile wash and pick over the spinach and watercress and slice the lettuce. Add these with the peas and broad beans to the pan, reserving a few leaves of watercress to garnish the soup. Cook for a further 10 minutes, then purée the soup in a liquidiser or food processor. It should be a luscious deep green.

IF SERVING IT HOT
Strain the soup back into the cleaned pan, taste for seasoning and reheat. Serve with a swirl of cream, a sprinkling of herbs and a watercress leaf on each plate. Tiny croûtons would also be good with this.

CROÛTONS
The old habit of serving sizzling hot croûtons with soup makes sense. It gives you something crisp to encounter while you are eating what is otherwise quite a lot of liquid. To make them, cut bread into ¼ inch (0.5 cm) cubes and fry these golden brown in butter and oil. Drain them well on kitchen paper and they can then be reheated; they should be served so hot that they sizzle when you spoon them into the hot soup.

IF SERVING IT COLD
Stir in the herbs and add the cream when the soup is cool. Serve at most lightly chilled and taste for flavour. Heavy chilling tends to make things tasteless.

Michael Mitchell's prize leeks, Dolton, North Devon

Summer Cucumber Soup with Dill

'Mercury hath the dominion of this plant and therefore to be sure it strengthens the brain. The dill . . . stayeth the hiccough, being boiled in wine, and but smelled unto being tied into a cloth. The seed is of more use than the leaves, and more effectual to digest raw and vicious humours, and is used in medicines that serve to expel wind, and the pains proceeding therefrom.'
Culpeper's COMPLETE HERBAL 1826

At one time it was considered very unhealthy to eat raw vegetables and even raw fruit — it was supposed to breed fevers and cucumbers were particularly suspect — so early recipes are for cooked cucumber served in a soup, a ragoût or as a vegetable. It is in fact excellent when cooked; I have combined cooked and raw together to get the nice flavour and velvetiness of cooked cucumber with the freshness of raw ones.

Serves 6

2 cucumbers

1 onion

1 pint (550 ml) chicken stock

1 glass dry white wine

1 bunch of herbs, including a sprig of dill

salt and freshly ground white pepper

¼ pint (150 ml) plain yoghurt

¼ pint (150 ml) soured cream (or more for a richer soup)

1 bunch of dill

squeeze of lemon juice (optional)

Peel and chop the cucumbers and onion. Put half the cucumber in a saucepan with the onion, chicken stock, white wine and bunch of herbs. Season and bring to the boil, skim and simmer for 20 minutes. Remove the bunch of herbs and liquidise the soup to a fine velvety purée.

Transfer it to a bowl and let it cool. Liquidise the remaining cucumber with the yoghurt and soured cream — do this very thoroughly to make certain the soup does not have too granular a texture. Mix this raw cucumber mixture into the soup and taste for seasoning — it needs quite a lot of salt. Stir in the chopped dill and chill the soup.

TO SERVE
Add a squeeze of lemon juice if you want a really sharp refreshing soup.

Soup tureens at Ponden Hall, Stanbury, Yorkshire

English Tomato and Mint Soup

'Sometimes, when I am working outside, I repair to the greenhouse for a tomato lunch, first providing myself with coffee, home-made bread, butter and salt. That's when you get to know just what perfection is in the tomato world.'
Constance Spry COME INTO THE GARDEN COOK 1942

It is crucial to use really good, ripe, rich tomatoes for this soup. I find a delicious alternative to fresh mint is leaves of fresh basil.

Serves 4

1½ lb (675 g) tomatoes, skinned

1 onion

1 small potato

1 leek

1 small stick of celery (optional)

1 oz (25 g) butter

½ pint (300 ml) chicken stock

a few sprigs of mint

up to ¼ pint (150 ml) double cream

salt and freshly ground pepper

Chop the onion, potato, leek and celery and soften them well in the butter but don't let them brown. Keeping two bright red ones aside, chop the tomatoes, crush them with a potato masher and add them to the other vegetables. Pour the stock into the pan, bring to the boil and leave to simmer for 20–25 minutes, stirring occasionally.

Meanwhile, concassé the raw tomatoes. To do this, cut them in half and squeeze out the pips, then cut the flesh into dice. Chop the mint.

When the soup is cooked, purée it in a mouli-légumes, liquidiser or food processor and strain through a sieve. Return the soup to the pan and add the double cream (single cream may curdle).

TO SERVE
Heat through, taste for seasoning and stir in the diced raw tomatoes and chopped mint.

Chicken à la Reine Soup

'According to traditions of the kitchen this soup owes its name to no less a personage than the wife of Henry IV, Margaret of Valois, who was said to be immensely fond of it.'
'The G.C.' ROUND THE TABLE 1873

This soup should be delicate, white and pure, with a good flavour of chicken.

Serves 4–6

legs, carcass and giblets of a chicken
    (the breasts can be used in another recipe),
    or better still use a whole boiling fowl

2 sticks of celery

2 onions

1 leek

8 black peppercorns

sprig of thyme

bunch of parsley

4 egg yolks

¼ pint (150 ml) double or single cream

salt

Slice the celery, onions and leek and put in a large pan with the carcass, legs and giblets (except the liver). Add the peppercorns and herbs, tied up in an outer leaf from the leek, and 4–5 pints (2.2–2.8 litres) cold water. Bring to a simmer and skim carefully; keep skimming from time to time as long as fat and impurities continue to rise to the top. Let the liquid just tremble for 2 hours, then strain it carefully through a clean tea towel and return it to the cleaned pan. Boil very slowly, uncovered, until reduced to 2 pints (1.1 litres). Taste for seasoning.

Beat the egg yolks with the cream and season lightly with salt. Ladle in a few tablespoons of the hot (not boiling) soup and stir well. Away from heat, add the egg and cream mixture to the pan, then return to a low heat and whisk until smooth. Do not allow to boil. Taste for seasoning.

Light Carrot Soup

The carrot ... 'was first generally cultivated in the reign of Queen Elizabeth, being introduced by the Flemings, who took refuge here from the persecutions of Philip II of Spain, and who, finding the soil about Sandwich particularly favourable for it, grew it there largely ... In the reign of James I, it became the fashion for ladies to use its feathery leaves in their head-dresses. A very charming, fern-like decoration may be obtained if the thick end of a large carrot be cut off and placed in a saucer of water in a warm place, when the young and delicate leaves soon begin to sprout and form a pretty tuft of verdant green, well worth the slight trouble entailed.'

Mrs M. Grieve A MODERN HERBAL 1931

I make this soup with young carrots which are somewhat mealy in texture if well cooked. Old carrots might not be so effective. As it contains no potatoes, this soup is very light, smooth and delicate. Half a teaspoon of cumin powder fried with the vegetables gives an interesting flavour, and you could spice it even more by using curry powder, and scattering chopped coriander over the soup before serving.

Serves 4

8 oz (225 g) new carrots
1 large onion
1 stick of celery
½ oz (15 g) butter
½ inch (1 cm) piece fresh ginger, peeled
½ chilli, stem and seeds removed
1 pint (550 ml) best home-made chicken stock
½ pint (300 ml) milk
salt
dash of cream

Clean the carrots and cut them up. Chop the onion and celery and soften them gently in butter for several minutes. Slice the ginger and chilli, then add the carrots, ginger and chilli to the pan and stir them round for a minute. Add the chicken stock and simmer until everything is very tender, about 25 minutes. Purée in a food processor, liquidiser or mouli-légumes and return the soup to the pan. Add the milk and season to taste.

TO SERVE
Heat through and serve with a dash of cream or a thin trickle of cream dribbled over the top of the soup in a criss-cross pattern.

Spong's rotary knife-cleaner

Mushroom Soup

This recipe, like most soup recipes, is much improved by the use of good chicken stock made from the remains of a roast chicken; a stock cube of course will do, but leaves the soup somehow rather thin. You can alter the richness by adding more or less cream and more or less nutmeg. It is equally delicious either served hot or chilled — a rare, soft dove colour, and very fine. You can make this even more velvety by doubling the quantity of mushrooms and leaving out the potatoes entirely. A few wild mushrooms, ceps, shaggy ink caps, parasols or St George's mushrooms give it a more 'gamey' flavour. Freshly chopped chervil is the perfect herb to complement the flavour of this soup.

Serves 4 – 6

8 oz (225 g) mushrooms

1 large onion (plus 2 shallots if these are available)

8 oz (225 g) potatoes

1½ oz (40 g) butter

1½ pints (850 ml) chicken stock (or 1 pint/550 ml chicken stock and ½ pint/300 ml creamy milk)

freshly ground nutmeg

salt and freshly ground pepper

3–4 tbsp cream

Peel and chop the onion, shallots and potatoes coarsely and soften them in the butter over a gentle heat for 15 minutes, stirring them round occasionally. Coarsely chop the mushrooms, add them and let them wilt and soften in the butter. Then add the stock, and a seasoning of plenty of nutmeg, plenty of pepper and salt to taste.

Simmer the soup for 20 minutes or until everything is cooked, then allow it to cool a little before you purée it in a liquidiser or food processor. Add the milk at this point if you are using it, and taste for seasoning.

TO SERVE
Either reheat, stir in the cream and serve hot, or let it cool and chill thoroughly.

Emerald Spinach Soup

There was a Young Lady of Poole,
Whose soup was excessively cool;
So she put it to boil
By the aid of some oil
That ingenious young lady of Poole.
from THE COMPLETE NONSENSE OF EDWARD LEAR

Cooking the spinach in butter rather than in the soup itself gives this a particularly good, velvety texture and deep green colour.

Serves 4–6

1 lb (450 g) spinach

1 onion

1 shallot

1 leek

1 potato

2 oz (50 g) butter

1 small glass dry white wine (3 fl oz/75 ml)

2 pints (1.1 litres) chicken stock

salt, pepper and nutmeg

2½ fl oz (60 ml) whipped cream

Wash and pick over the spinach and leave it in a colander to drain. Keep 6 young leaves aside and shred them. Chop the onion, shallot and leek finely. Peel and grate the potato. Heat half the butter and soften the chopped onion, shallot and leek; add the grated potato, glass of wine and the stock and cook gently for 20 minutes until tender. Season with salt, pepper and nutmeg. Keep on one side.

Now cook the spinach in the remaining butter until it wilts down — adding it to the pan a few handfuls at a time. Add it to the soup, bring to the boil for 1 minute then liquidise. Serve hot with a few shreds of spinach and a dollop of whipped cream on each bowl.

Yellow Pea Soup

As an alternative, this delicious, encouraging winter soup can be made with dried green peas.

Serves 6

10 oz (300 g) yellow split peas

a ham bone with a bit of ham on it (or a raw gammon knuckle, soaked for several hours)

1 onion, chopped

1 stick of celery, chopped

1 bayleaf

½ oz (15 g) butter

½ oz (15 g) flour

¼ pint (150 ml) milk

¼ pint (150 ml) single cream

salt and freshly ground pepper

Soak the peas overnight in 1¾ pints (1 litre) water. (Or if you are in a hurry, use the quick method — cover the peas with 1¾ pints (1 litre) cold water, bring to the boil and cook for 5 minutes; cover the pan, remove from the heat and allow to cool.) If necessary, soak the ham bone — an uncooked smoked knuckle will need overnight soaking, a cooked ham bone will not.

Put the peas and their soaking water, the onion, celery, ham bone and bayleaf in a large pan. Cover with 2¼ pints (1.3 litres) water and simmer for 1½–2 hours, until the peas are soft. Remove the bone and bayleaf and sieve the soup through a mouli-légumes or purée it in a food processor or liquidiser and then sieve.

Make a sauce with the butter, flour and milk. Melt the butter in a small pan, stir in the flour and gradually add the milk. Cook over a low heat, stirring until smooth and thickened. Stir the sauce into the soup, taste for seasoning and add half the cream. Remove the ham from the bone and cut it in small pieces; add these to the soup.

TO SERVE
Heat through and serve with a swirl of cream and some very coarsely ground pepper on each bowlful.

Curried Lentil Soup with Cream

This is a sort of Mulligatawny but rather more subtle. As an alternative it can be made with other varieties of lentil, or with split yellow peas.

Serves 6

FOR THE SPECIAL STOCK

1 lb (450 g) stewing beef, such as shin

2 carrots

1 onion, stuck with a clove

1 stick of celery

1 bayleaf

1 sprig of lovage

½ tsp peppercorns

FOR THE SOUP

8 oz (225 g) small split orange lentils

1 carrot

1 stick of celery

1 onion

4 cloves garlic

1½ oz (40 g) butter

1 tbsp curry powder (can be home-made)

3 pints (1.7 litres) stock — see above

1 tsp curry paste

4 cardamom seeds

salt

¼ pint (150 ml) cream

milk to taste

chopped fresh coriander leaves

SPECIAL STOCK
Make the special stock if you have time as it gives the soup a most delicious flavour. Cover the ingredients with water, bring to the boil, skim and simmer for 3–4 hours. Strain and make up to 3 pints (1.7 litres) with water.

SOUP

Chop the vegetables and slice the cloves of garlic. Melt the butter in a large pan and put in the lentils and chopped vegetables, garlic and curry powder. Stir them round for a few minutes, but don't allow to brown.

Add the stock, curry paste and cardamom seeds. Stir and simmer for $\frac{3}{4}$–1 hour until the lentils and vegetables are completely tender. Purée in a mouli-légumes or food processor — if using the latter, strain the soup through a sieve.

TO SERVE

Add the cream and enough milk to give it the consistency you like. Taste for seasoning and serve very hot with a teaspoon of cream in each soup plate, and if possible a scattering of chopped green coriander.

NOTE

If you care to make the garam masala on page 146, it has exactly the right flavour for this soup. Otherwise 1 tsp ground coriander and $\frac{1}{2}$ tsp ground cumin can be added to an ordinary curry powder and will improve the taste.

Hotch Potch

which 'it must be remembered should be more of a stodge than a broth.'
Edward Spencer CAKES AND ALE 1897

Hotch potch is one of those timeless concoctions in which every kind of vegetable available is thrown into a pot, with some meat if you happen to have any, covered with water and stewed over the fire. It dates from the very earliest times when meals had to be cooked all in one container over the hearth.

Serves 4–6

| 2 onions |
| 2 carrots |
| 1 slice of white turnip |
| 3 pints (1.7 litres) lamb broth — from a boiled leg of lamb, made with scrag or middle neck or, as last resort, beef stock cubes |
| 1 lettuce |
| 1 small green cabbage |
| 8 oz (225 g) shelled green peas |
| 1 tbsp chopped parsley |
| salt and coarsely ground black pepper |

Cut the onions, carrots and turnip into small pieces and put them in a pan with the broth. Bring to the boil and simmer with a tilted lid on the pan for half an hour. Add the lettuce and the cabbage cut up small and simmer for a further half an hour. Add the peas, cook uncovered for 10 minutes and then add the parsley and a good quantity of very coarse and freshly ground black pepper. Serve hot with plenty of bread and butter.

VARIATIONS

If you like to make the soup up to the point where you add the peas and let it get cold, then reheat it, add the peas and finish cooking it as before, this makes it even more delicious. It is very good, slightly lighter than the original versions because no meat is actually cooked with the soup. If you do want to put in some lamb neck chops or even cutlets, remember to skim the soup very carefully, and add a little more liquid if necessary, to make up for what is lost during the skimming.

You can add any of the following vegetables without changing the character of the soup — cucumber, celery, cauliflower (I'm not personally very keen on this), asparagus, leeks, broad beans, soaked dried peas, rice or barley.

Parslied Barley Broth

'In cold, hard winters soup was made twice a week in the vicarage washing-copper, and the cans of all comers were filled without question. It was . . . rich and thick with pearl barley and lean beef gobbets and golden carrot rings and fat little dumplings — so solidly good that a spoon would stand in it upright.'
Flora Thompson LARK RISE TO CANDLEFORD 1939

Originally this soup would have been made with a piece of beef or mutton cooked in with the vegetables. If you prefer to use the old method a well-trimmed piece of neck of lamb started half an hour before the vegetables go in, and well-skimmed, gives a particularly good flavour. If you want to add dumplings, use the recipe on page 59.

Serves 6 or more

4 oz (100 g) yellow split peas

2 medium onions

3 carrots

1 small turnip

1 small swede (optional)

3 oz (75 g) pearl barley

3 pints (1.7 litres) beef or lamb stock (or use stock cubes)

1 young leek

1 tender white inner stick of celery

1 small slender parsnip (optional)

¼ fresh green cabbage

salt and freshly ground pepper

2–3 tbsp freshly chopped parsley

Soak the split peas overnight or this can be done quickly by putting them in a saucepan of cold water, bringing this to the boil and simmering for 5 minutes; then remove them from the heat, cover the pan and leave to cool. By the time the peas are cool they are soft enough to cook. Drain off the soaking water and they will be considerably more digestible.

Cut the onions, carrots, turnip and swede into small pieces and put them into a saucepan with the soaked peas and barley; cover with the stock, bring to the boil, skim well and simmer for 1 hour.

Meanwhile, slice the leek into halves lengthwise and then into small pieces. Cut the celery into little crescents; cut the parsnip into quarters and then slice it. Add these to the soup and cook for a further 15-20 minutes.

Remove the stalk from the cabbage and slice into small and manageable strips — long strips are to be avoided as they hang over the side of the spoon and drip everywhere. Add the cabbage to the soup. Simmer until all the vegetables are tender, adding more stock if necessary. Taste for seasoning and give the soup a good stir.

TO SERVE
Sprinkle with plenty of chopped parsley and coarsely ground black pepper at the last minute and serve very hot with brown bread and butter. The soup reheats well but becomes rather thick — add more stock if necessary.

English Palestine Soup

Palestine soup is so called because the English, never very good at foreign languages, thought *girasole*, the Italian name for artichokes, was Jerusalem and that they must have come from there. This soup would not go down very well with French visitors, particularly if you told them what it was made of, as they only use *topinambours* to feed pigs and chickens.

Serves 4

1 lb (450 g) Jerusalem artichokes

8 oz (225 g) potatoes

1 pint (550 ml) best home-made chicken stock

1 large onion (8 oz/225 g)

1 stick of celery

½ oz (15 g) butter

½–¾ pint (300–425 ml) milk

salt and freshly ground pepper

few tbsp cream

chopped parsley or mint

Peel the artichokes and potatoes and cut them into small pieces. Put them in a bowl of cold water as you do so to prevent them from becoming discoloured. Heat the stock.

Chop the onion and celery and soften them in the butter, without letting them brown. Add the rest of the vegetables, drained, and cook gently in the butter for a few minutes before adding the hot stock and a pinch of salt. Simmer for 20–25 minutes until both artichokes and potatoes are completely tender.

Sieve the soup through a mouli-légumes or, if you prefer, purée it in a food processor or liquidiser. I personally prefer the texture of a sieved soup, it is less bland. Add a nut of butter and enough milk to give the soup the right consistency. I like it rather thick. Heat it through and taste for seasoning.

TO SERVE
Add freshly ground pepper, spoon in the cream and sprinkle with chopped parsley or mint.

Potato Soup with Parsley

A little nutmeg is quite a good addition to this favourite old standby.

Serves 6

1 lb (450 g) potatoes

1 lb (450 g) onions

2 rashers bacon

2 pints (1.1 litres) chicken stock

salt and freshly ground pepper

½ pint (300 ml) milk

¼ pint (150 ml) double cream

3–4 tbsp chopped parsley

Peel and chop the potatoes and onions. Cook the rashers of bacon for 5 minutes in the stock, then remove them and set them to one side. Put the potatoes and onions into the pan with the stock and season with salt and pepper. Bring to the boil and simmer for 20 minutes.

Purée the soup in a mouli-légumes (don't use a food processor or liquidiser as these tend to make the potatoes gluey). Cut the bacon into strips. Return the soup to the cleaned pan, add the strips of bacon and milk.

TO SERVE
Heat through, add the cream and stir in the parsley. Heat again, taste for seasoning and serve hot. You can also serve croûtons — little cubes of fried bread — with this soup (see page 12).

In the kitchen at Great Dixter, East Sussex

Vichyssoise

This is a favourite old mid-Atlantic classic, said to have been invented on board a transatlantic liner. It is as good hot as cold.

Serves 4–6

1 lb (450 g) leeks

1 onion

8 oz (225 g) potatoes

1 stick of celery

few sprigs of watercress

1¾ pints (1 litre) chicken stock

½ glass dry white wine

salt and freshly ground white pepper

1 egg yolk

¼ pint (150 ml) double cream

a few leaves of tarragon or a bunch of chives

Prepare and cut up the vegetables and wash and trim the watercress. Put the leeks, onion, potatoes and celery into a pan with the stock and white wine. Bring to the boil, season and cook for 10 minutes, then add the leeks and watercress and cook until tender, about 15 minutes is enough if the leeks are small.

Purée the soup through the fine blade of a mouli-légumes or process in a liquidiser or food processor and then sieve. Return the soup to the pan.

Put the egg yolk in a bowl and whisk it with a ladleful of the hot (not boiling) soup. Return this mixture to the pan and stir it into the rest of the soup together with about 2½ fl oz (65 ml) of the cream.

Cool the mixture and then chill, covered.

TO SERVE
Give the soup a good stir, season and serve each bowl with a zig-zag pattern of cream in the centre — drizzle it on with a spoon in a thin stream — and two tarragon leaves, or a sprinkling of chopped fresh chives.

Spinach Soufflé with Anchovy Sauce

This is my version of the favourite dish at Langan's Brasserie in Stratton Street off Piccadilly. If you are not used to making soufflés then Julia Child's chapter in *Mastering the Art of French Cooking* makes you an immediate expert. This is a shortened version based on her method.

Serves 4

FOR THE SOUFFLÉ

a little butter and grated Parmesan to prepare the soufflé dish

8 oz (225 g) puréed fresh spinach (or frozen)

2¼ oz (55g) butter

salt, freshly ground pepper and plenty of freshly grated nutmeg

1½ oz (40 g) flour

½ pint (300 ml) boiling milk

4 egg yolks

5 egg whites

2 oz (50 g) grated Emmenthal cheese

FOR THE ANCHOVY SAUCE

4 oz (100 g) unsalted butter

2 egg yolks

4 tbsp double cream

juice of ½ lemon

2 oz (50 g) tin anchovies in oil, well drained and chopped

TO MAKE THE ANCHOVY SAUCE

Cut the butter up into small cubes. Put the egg yolks, cream, lemon juice and anchovies in the top of a double boiler or saucepan over hot water. Stir over a medium heat and gradually add the butter a piece at a time, letting each piece melt before adding another. Keep stirring over a low heat — don't let the water even simmer — until the sauce is creamy and the anchovies have dissolved.

Keep the sauce warm over hot water.

TO MAKE THE SOUFFLÉ

First prepare a 2 pint (1.1 litre) soufflé dish by rubbing the inside well with soft butter and then dusting it with grated Parmesan.

Put the spinach into a saucepan with a nut of the butter, salt, pepper and plenty of nutmeg, and let it cook gently until all the liquid in it has evaporated.

Melt the remaining butter in a medium saucepan, stir in the flour, let it cook for a minute or two then remove from the heat and add all the boiling milk. Stir rapidly and when it is a smoothish mixture, cook over a medium heat, stirring for a minute or two, then remove from the heat and stir in the spinach.

Now add the egg yolks one at a time, beating them in. Taste the mixture, adding more salt, pepper and nutmeg if necessary. Preheat the oven to 375°F (190°C, Gas 5).

Put the egg whites into a large, spotlessly clean bowl. Whisk them to a firm snow; to test, pull the whisk out vertically and up-end it. The peak should sag but not flop. Fold a quarter of the egg whites into the spinach mixture, add all but 1 tablespoon of the Emmenthal cheese, then add the rest of the egg whites and gently fold them in with a spatula. Don't overwork the mixture, it must stay light and airy.

Transfer it to a soufflé dish and sprinkle with the remaining Emmenthal cheese. Run your thumb round the rim of the dish and smooth the edge away, this helps the soufflé to rise straight up. Put it into the middle of the oven. Cook for 20 minutes then have a look at it. If it is too wobbly, give it another 5 minutes. It should look like a classic soufflé, and be rather quivery, not set right through. Serve at once with the warm anchovy sauce.

ALTERNATIVE

You can serve a tomato sauce, well flavoured with chives, instead of the anchovy sauce.

Hole Farm, North Devon

Egg Mousse

This is the essential and original recipe for an egg mousse. You can add, with the herbs, cooked prawns dusted with cayenne pepper, or cooked shelled mussels, which should be arranged on the bottom of the soufflé dish, on top of the layer of hard-boiled eggs. Plain or elaborate, it is a delicate summer dish, rather suitable for ladies' lunches, or as a first course at dinner.

Serves 6–8

6 eggs
bunch of fresh tarragon
1 pint (550 ml) chicken consommé (bought or home-made)
4 leaves or ½ oz (15 g) gelatine (enough to set 1 pint/550 ml)
bunch of fresh chives
1 tbsp sherry
good double shake of Tabasco sauce
¼ pint (150 ml) single cream
¼ pint (150 ml) double cream
a few leaves of flat parsley or coriander for decoration

Hard-boil the eggs, and run them under cold water to cool. Strip the tarragon leaves from their stalks and put the stalks into ¼ pint (150 ml) consommé; heat it in a small pan, infuse for 5 minutes to allow it to take up the tarragon flavour and then use it to dissolve the gelatine. Strain it, and combine it with the rest of the consommé. Keep a scant ¼ pint (150 ml) of this on one side, apart from the rest.

Chop the tarragon leaves and chives quite small and stir them into the ¾ pint (425 ml) consommé. Allow it to cool but not quite set, then add the sherry and Tabasco.

Put the two creams into a bowl and whip until thick but not very stiff; stir into the tarragon and chive-flavoured consommé. Taste the mixture for seasoning.

Slice the hard-boiled eggs, keep 3 slices for decoration and put the rest into the bottom of a 2½ pint (1.4 litre) soufflé dish. Pour on the mousse mixture and allow to chill in the refrigerator. When it is firm, arrange the 3 slices of egg in the middle with flat parsley or coriander leaves all round — dip these in the remaining consommé to keep them in place. Then chill again and lastly pour over the ¼ pint (150 ml) reserved consommé, which should be cool but still liquid. Chill.

TO SERVE
Serve with granary bread and butter and a glass of cold Chablis.

Baked Eggs

'It's very easy to talk', said Mrs Mantalini. 'Not so easy when one is eating a demnition egg,' replied Mr Mantalini; 'for the yolk runs down the waistcoat, and yolk of egg does not match any waistcoat but a yellow waistcoat, demmit'
Charles Dickens NICHOLAS NICKLEBY 1838

The most important thing about these delicate eggs is that they should be soft enough to drip down your waistcoat; they are no good once they have gone hard. Eat these delicious creamy eggs plain as a breakfast dish or, with something underneath, as a first course. In the same way as there are endless different omelettes, there are many ways to make baked eggs. They are particularly good with prawns, flaked smoked haddock or mushrooms cooked in butter. You can also try them with cooked chicken livers or little strips of ham dusted with Parmesan cheese. Chives are very good with either of these.

Serves 2 or 4

4 free-range eggs
½ oz (15 g) salted butter
4 tbsp cream
cayenne pepper

Preheat the oven to either 425°F (220°C, Gas 7) or 350°F (180°C, Gas 4). Butter 4 small cocottes generously. Break an egg into each and pour 1 tbsp cream over each one. Dust with cayenne pepper and bake at the high temperature for 8 minutes or the lower temperature for 12 minutes. Let each person put their own salt on; if you put salt on before cooking it makes spots on the eggs. If using a filling, put it in the bottom of the cocotte with the butter, then break the egg on top.

ANOTHER SORT OF BAKED EGGS
Instead of putting cream on top, put a nut of butter underneath the egg. It will come up the sides of the egg making it slightly 'fried' round the edges, very good for breakfast.

Peppered Scrambled Eggs with Smoked Salmon

Serves 6

3 oz (75 g) butter

12 free-range eggs

24–30 black peppercorns

about 8 oz (225 g) freshly cut Scotch smoked salmon, sliced into 6 slices

1 tsp salt

Serve this on cold plates and keep the salmon to one side to leave room for the eggs — if you put it over the top of hot eggs it will go oily and then start to lose its translucence. Have 6 plates ready with their slice of salmon before you start the eggs.

Half-melt the butter over a low heat in a good thick saucepan, enamelled iron or heavy stainless steel. Remove from the heat and allow to cool, then add the eggs one at a time. Season with up to 1 tsp salt, less if using salted butter.

Pound the peppercorns roughly in a mortar with a pestle and add them to the eggs. Return the pan to the heat and stir, scraping the bottom of the pan continuously with a wooden spoon. The eggs will start to set and form lumps. Keep going until the eggs are about two-thirds set, then remove the pan from the heat and finish, still stirring, in a cooling pan so that you do not have any overcooked bits.

When the eggs are soft and creamy all through, divide them out on to the plates alongside the smoked salmon and serve at once with more pepper. Do not serve lemon with this.

ALTERNATIVE

As an extremely delicious alternative, serve fillets of smoked eel with the scrambled eggs. Allow two 4 inch (10 cm) pieces of fillet to each person and put them in a cross over the top of the scrambled eggs — as they are thicker they can stand up to the heat of the eggs without spoiling.

Devilled Chicken Livers

Serves 6

2 lb (900 g) chicken livers

1–2 tbsp Dijon mustard

generous shake of Tabasco sauce, to taste

generous shake of Worcestershire sauce

squeeze of lemon juice

1 tsp coarsely crushed black peppercorns

1 onion, finely chopped

2 oz (50 g) butter and 2 tbsp oil for frying

3–4 tsp flour

1 wine glass dry sherry

salt and freshly ground pepper

Drain and clean the chicken livers and put them in a bowl. Mix together $\frac{1}{2}$ tbsp mustard, the Tabasco, Worcestershire sauce and lemon juice and spread it over the chicken livers with your hands. Stir in the peppercorns and leave for up to an hour.

Brown half the chopped onion in half the butter and oil; if you try to cook all the chicken livers at once you will find the juices will run out and they will not brown. So, cook them in two or even more batches, adding the remaining onion, and placing the livers in the very hot pan with your fingers so that they do not overlap. Let them fry quite fast for a couple of minutes with the onions, then turn them once and cook for a minute or two more, adding the remaining butter and oil as necessary. Sprinkle with salt and flour, stir quickly round then add sherry and salt and pepper. Sizzle for a minute or so and then taste the juices, adding more mustard, Tabasco and Worcestershire sauce to your taste.

Poached Eggs with Anchovies

*'Butter squares of crisply fried bread with anchovy
butter (which is merely butter mixed with anchovy
paste); place a perfectly good poached egg on each
square, then lay two or three strips of filleted
anchovy prettily crosswise on each egg.'*
Atherton Fleming GOURMET'S BOOK OF FOOD AND
DRINK 1933

Welsh Rabbit

I like best G.M. Boumphrey's description of Welsh
Rabbit from his *Weekend Cookery Book*. He
regards the dish as a savoury but it also makes a
good quick lunch or supper. He would have the
toast trimmed of its crust and, rather eccentrically,
buttered on both sides.

*'Welsh Rabbit is best made . . . by grating the
cheese, adding to it a little dry mustard, salt, if
needed and pepper, and mixing it to a paste with
beer or milk and a suspicion of Worcester Sauce.
Cover the buttered toast with this to the depth of
about ¼ inch and brown in the oven or under a grill.
Sprinkle with tabasco or cayenne and serve very
hot.'*

To which I would add, use at least 1–1½ oz (25–40 g)
good mature Cheddar or Lancashire cheese for each
piece of bread, toast the bread only on one side and
put the cheese on the untoasted side.

I prefer made mustard to dry mustard and for a
change use chive mustard which goes well with the
cheese. Serve with red tomato chutney (page 148).

Welsh Rabbit of Stilton and Walnuts

People are often left with large amounts of Stilton to
eat their way through after Christmas; this is one
good way of doing it. Not everybody knows how
tasty Stilton is served hot, melting and overflowing
the edges of a piece of fresh toast. To make this
extremely delicious dish, toast a piece of bread on
one side, butter the untoasted side lightly and crumble 1 oz (25 g) Stilton over it. Scatter the contents of
three fresh walnuts over the top. Grill very gently
until the Stilton starts to run and serve at once.

The cheese stall, Barnstaple Pannier Market, North Devon

'TO MAKE AN ENGLISH RABBIT
*Toast a slice of bread brown on both sides, then lay
it on a Plate before the Fire, pour a Glass of red
Wine over it, and let it soak the Wine up; then cut
some Cheese very thin, and lay it very thick over the
Bread, and put it in a Tin Oven before the Fire, and
it will be toasted and browned presently. Serve it
away hot.'*
Hannah Glasse THE ART OF COOKERY MADE PLAIN
AND EASY 1758

Stilton on sale at Paxton and Whitfield, Jermyn Street, London

Parmesan Fingers

'Cut stale white bread into fingers. Soak in cream. Then roll in grated Parmesan cheese and pepper and pat with a knife so that cheese sticks well. Butter a baking sheet and bake in a very hot oven and turn when one side is brown, so that the other side browns. Serve very hot.'
Mrs Winston Churchill

These are extremely good, instead of bought cocktail biscuits and junk food. The recipe came from *A Medley of Recipes* by Dorothy Allhusen published in 1936 before Winston Churchill had led the country through the Second World War. It is nice to think of Clementine, while she was living quietly at Chartwell, having interest enough to give her recipes to friends.

Curried Cheese Straws

Makes about 20

Make half the quantity of rough puff pastry (page 138) and, while you are rolling and turning it, sprinkle each layer with a little finely grated Parmesan mixed with curry powder — use 1 oz (25 g) Parmesan and 1 tsp curry powder, altogether. After the final folding, roll out to $\frac{1}{4}$ inch (6 mm) thick in the normal way, cut into strips about $\frac{1}{2}$ inch (1 cm) wide, twist the strips and put them on a wetted baking sheet allowing room to expand. Chill.

Preheat the oven to 400°F (200°C, Gas 6) and bake for 8–10 minutes or until crisp, light and brown. The straws burn very suddenly so take care over the last few minutes of cooking.

Seafood Salad

A fairly recent English invention was the prawn cocktail, which soon became a very bad and very boring dish, so I have revived and improved it. The sauce made in this recipe can be used with crab on its own, prawns on their own, or with lobster. It can be prepared the day before and assembled on the day, shortly before serving.

Serves 8

| 1 lb (450 g) frozen raw Chinese prawns (small, in shells), defrosted |
| 2 lb (1 kg) scallops out of shells (about 2 scallops per person) |
| 2 large tomatoes |
| 1 curly endive |
| 4 oz (100 g) or more lamb's lettuce or corn salad |

FOR THE SAUCE

| 2 egg yolks |
| 1 generous tsp Dijon mustard |
| 1 lemon |
| salt |
| $\frac{1}{2}$ pint (300 ml) salad oil (I use sunflower) |
| 2 tsp red wine or a little more |
| $\frac{1}{2}$ tsp tomato purée |
| 2–3 shakes Tabasco sauce |

COOKING THE SEAFOOD

Bring a wide pan of well-salted water to the boil, drop in the defrosted prawns and simmer gently for 2–3 minutes. Lift them out, and poach the scallops gently in the same liquid for 2–3 minutes until just opaque. Scoop out, and allow to cool.

Skin the tomatoes, cut in half and remove the seeds. Cut into small cubes. Wash the endive and lamb's lettuce carefully and shake dry. Choose only the best bits. Shell the prawns. Cut the scallops in half horizontally.

SAUCE

Beat the egg yolks, mustard, lemon juice and salt together with a whisk. When the mixture is light and creamy pour the oil in steadily from a jug in a thin stream, whisking all the time, until all the oil is incorporated. Add the red wine, tomato purée and Tabasco and whisk again.

TO SERVE

Arrange the shelled prawns, scallops, curly endive, lamb's lettuce and chopped tomato prettily on eight dishes. Serve with the cocktail sauce.

Potted Shrimps or Prawns

This will keep well for a week in the refrigerator and is improved after a few days. Lobster or crab can be potted in exactly the same way.

Makes 6 small pots

1 lb (450 g) shelled shrimps or prawns, fresh or frozen

8 oz (225 g) unsalted butter

½ tsp freshly pounded mace

¼ tsp cayenne pepper (or more to taste)

¼ tsp freshly ground black pepper

salt if necessary

If the shrimps have been frozen, let them defrost completely in a sieve so that any melted ice drains off. They must be as dry as possible.

Melt the butter in a small pan with a pouring lip, at the lowest temperature possible. Let it sit over this heat for 30 minutes until all the whitish curds, which are the milk solids, have formed a layer at the bottom of the pan and the oiled butter is quite clear.

Put the shrimps or prawns in a bowl and mix in the seasonings with your fingers. Pour on the clear melted butter, leaving all the white solids in the pan. Wash out the solids and return clarified butter and shellfish to the pan and let it sit over the same very low heat for a further ½ hour. Divide the shrimps or prawns and butter between six small pots and press them down under the butter. Allow to set. Serve at room temperature with hot toast.

Rocks at Bucks Mills, North Devon

Prawn Paste

This is an old family recipe of Theodora Fitzgibbon's, from her book *Irish Traditional Food*. I found I could make it in a food processor, which cuts out the original laborious pounding, and I used anchovy paste from a tube rather than the original anchovy essence. It keeps well in the fridge, and is very good for picnics, or as a first course. It is more like a pâté than a paste.

Serves 6–8

12 oz (350 g) cooked prawns in their shells

salt

12 oz (350 g) fresh haddock fillets

pinch of ground mace

pinch of cayenne pepper

1 heaped tsp anchovy paste

8 oz (225 g) softened butter

Shell the prawns and boil the shells for 20 minutes in enough water to cover, mashing them well with a wooden spoon. Strain them, taste the liquid, add salt and a little more water if necessary and cook the haddock in this prawn stock for 15 minutes. Remove the haddock. Strain again, keeping a tablespoon of this concentrated liquid.

Purée the haddock in a liquidiser or food processor with the mace, cayenne, anchovy paste and a little of the cooking liquid. When the mixture is cool add all but a tablespoon of the butter and purée the mixture until smooth. Chop the prawns and stir them into the mixture, heat it gently for a couple of minutes and then press into a deep dish or pot. Melt the remaining butter and pour it over the top. Chill until set.

TO SERVE
Slice and serve with pale, crisp, inner lettuce leaves.

Salmon Mousse

You can make either a rough or smooth mousse. Perhaps a rough mousse is more satisfactory as a main course, and a very fine one as a first course.

Serves 6

1 lb (450 g) tail end of salmon, poached (page 34)

½ tsp paprika

¼ tsp Tabasco sauce

¼ pint (150 ml) home-made mayonnaise

½ oz (15 g) powdered gelatine

¼ pint (150 ml) water in which the salmon was cooked, or fish or chicken stock

¼ pint (150 ml) whipped cream

salt and freshly ground white pepper

2 egg whites

leaves of fresh dill, tarragon or parsley

Chop the salmon fairly finely, reserving 5 large, even flakes for decorating. Mix the paprika and Tabasco into the mayonnaise. Melt the gelatine in the hot stock, allow it to cool, then stir it gradually into the mayonnaise to make a smooth liquid. Stir in the salmon. At this point, if you are making a smooth mousse, purée the mixture thoroughly to a pink mousseline using a liquidiser or food processor.

Add the whipped cream, and season generously. Whip the egg whites to a firm snow and fold carefully into the salmon mixture. Transfer to a 1½ pint (850 ml) soufflé dish and decorate the top with the flakes of salmon arranged like a geranium flower, putting herb leaves in between the petals. Cover and chill until set.

TO SERVE
As a starter, serve with hot toast or brown bread and butter, and quartered lemons or a bowl of mayonnaise with chopped dill and parsley stirred into it. As a main course, serve with a salad of lettuce hearts, fennel and thinly sliced radishes.

This mixture can also be divided among 6 or 8 small cocottes, and sprinkled with chopped dill.

FISH AND SHELLFISH

I have recently been cooking more and more fish; it has become a new pleasure with me, and if I can find some new source of supply or a variety that I have not tried before, I feel the real thrill of the chase. It started when I suddenly found that handling really fresh fish and shellfish was actually perfectly agreeable, a discovery which came with eating, and then helping to prepare, sashimi — a Japanese dish of raw salmon, tuna, turbot, sole, squid or even mackerel. We did the mackerel like this in Scotland, when the children were hauling far too many lines of these prolific fish into the rowing boat every day, and we were running out of enthusiasm for eating them cooked in oatmeal. They were exquisite raw, straight from an icy cold sea-loch, beautifully fresh and smelling only of the sea.

After this holiday the preparation of fish of all sorts lost its difficulties for me. I clean them quickly on a newspaper — not the favoured chopping board — or under the cold tap with a sieve underneath it to catch the bits. It takes seconds and doesn't make you or the house smell of fish.

Many English people, however, prefer to buy and cook emasculated frozen fish to avoid the trouble of preparation. They are doing themselves out of a fascinating side of a cook's life: all the French chefs I have ever interviewed, from the Troisgros Frères, to Michel Guérard and Alain Chapel, say that their favourite branch of cooking is the cooking of fish, and I agree.

Staithes, Yorkshire

32

Poached Salmon with New Potatoes and Hollandaise Sauce

The inevitable British lunch in May or June.

Serves 6

3 lb (1.3 kg) tail end of fresh salmon

salt

5 bayleaves

1–2 tbsp peppercorns

2 glasses dry white wine

FOR THE EASY HOLLANDAISE SAUCE

2 egg yolks

5 tbsp single cream

½–1 tsp white wine vinegar

pinch of salt

3–4 oz (75–100 g) butter

fresh tarragon

SAUCE

Beat the egg yolks, half the cream, vinegar and a pinch of salt in the top of a double-boiler and stir over very hot, but not boiling water, until the mixture thickens slightly. Start adding the butter in small pieces, stirring each one into the velvety yellow mixture until it has completely dissolved and disappeared before adding the next. Remove the pan from the heat from time to time to make sure it does not overheat.

Stir in the remaining cream and a little chopped tarragon if you like. Keep warm away from the heat, but over hot water, until needed, stirring from time to time.

COOKING THE SALMON

Put the bayleaves, peppercorns, salt, white wine and plenty of water into your pan and heat gently to blood heat. Slide in the salmon or lower it in in a cloth if you are not using a fish kettle with a removable rack. You will then be able to lift it out without breaking it.

Bring to simmering point and simmer gently for 8

minutes per 1 lb (450 g) and 8 minutes over (if you like it rather firm allow a further minute or two). Lift it out carefully (or let it cool a little in the water if you are going to eat it cold).

TO SERVE

Decorate the fish with slices of lemon and sprigs of tarragon. Taste the sauce and adjust the seasoning. Serve with new potatoes.

Salmon Trout with Horseradish

Many fishmongers are now selling large farmed trout fed with special food which makes their flesh pink. Unfortunately they are often passed off as salmon trout, but are coarser and rather soft and boring to eat — so it is prudent to ask for wild salmon trout and ask about its origins.

Ask the fishmonger to clean the fish, paying great attention to the dark channel along the inside of the spine, which is bitter and spoils the look of the fish.

Serves 6

1 whole salmon trout weighing 3–4 lb (1.3–1.8 kg)

salt

a little oil

2 tbsp dry white wine

Preheat the oven to 325°F (170°C, Gas 3).

Rub the fish with salt inside and out, and sprinkle with a little oil. Place a large piece of foil on a table or work surface and bend up the sides and ends. Put in the fish, pour in the wine and fold the foil into a parcel. Bake for 30–40 minutes.

Pierce the trout behind the head with a knife to see if it is cooked. A compact fish will take longer than a long thin one. When it is ready, remove it carefully, slide it on to a long dish and let it cool.

TO SERVE

Serve with Lady Sysonby's horseradish sauce (see page 144).

Salmon trout cooked in foil is also extremely good served hot; the most usual sauce and one of the best is hollandaise (left), but it is also rather good with a pink maltaise sauce — hollandaise sauce with the juice of blood oranges in it.

Salmon Fishcakes

Serves 4

1 lb (450 g) fresh salmon or leftover cooked salmon

3–4 mealy potatoes, medium size

½ pint (300 ml) milk

2 blades of mace

2 bayleaves

½ onion

salt and freshly ground pepper

cayenne pepper

2 oz (50 g) pepper

1½ oz (40 g) flour

2 tbsp cream

1 tsp white wine vinegar

chopped fresh dill or parsley

flour for shaping

oil and butter for frying

The fishcakes can be as rich and creamy or as filling as you like, according to how much potato you put into the mixture. Make it the day before or several hours in advance. First, cook the salmon, following either of the previous recipes.

Cook the potatoes in their skins in boiling salted water until very soft; drain, peel and mash them.

Meanwhile, make a very thick cream sauce. Heat the milk to boiling point and leave to infuse with the mace, bayleaves, and half an onion, and a generous seasoning of salt and cayenne pepper. Melt the butter in a small pan, stir in the flour and let it cook for a few minutes. Remove it from the heat, and let it cool a little, then strain on the milk and add any juices from the salmon. Stir well, return to the heat and cook until smooth and thick.

Add the cream, vinegar and chopped dill or parsley. Taste for seasoning and stir in the mashed potato — lightly but not too thoroughly — and lastly the skinned, boned and flaked salmon. Allow the mixture to cool and set for two hours if possible.

Shape into 8 patties with well-floured hands and fry over a medium heat in a little oil and butter until golden brown — turn them very carefully.

Serve with fried potatoes and quarters of lemon, and parsley sauce (page 143), if liked.

Netting salmon on the River Torridge, Bideford, North Devon

Salmon Kedgeree

Serves 4

8 oz (225 g) fresh salmon in a piece (leftover salmon is fine, or you can use tinned)

1 oz (25 g) butter

8 oz (225 g) Patna rice

salt and freshly ground pepper

3 large eggs

4 oz (100 g) frozen peas

¼ pint (150 ml) double cream

2 tbsp chopped parsley

A good traditional British way to cook a slice or cutlet of fish is to salt it and put it with a little butter — ½–1 oz (15–25 g) — between two plates. These are put over a pan of cooking rice (or potatoes or whatever it is) and the fish poaches gently in its own steam and juices. A slice of salmon weighing 8 oz (225 g) takes about the same time as the rice — about 15–20 minutes. You could also do it in a large double-boiler.

To cook the rice, rinse it and put it in a pan with ½ pint (300 ml) water and a generous pinch of salt. Bring it to the boil, stir it once and cover the pan. Simmer for 10–15 minutes, until all the water is absorbed and the rice is tender. Meanwhile hard-boil the eggs and cook the peas.

Fork the rice lightly, add 2 of the hard-boiled eggs chopped into large pieces, the peas and the flaked fish with its juices and butter. Fork together lightly and taste for seasoning. The kedgeree can be heated again in the top of a double-boiler if necessary and then kept hot for half an hour or so over gently simmering water. Add more butter to taste.

Bring the cream to the boil in a small pan, season it with salt and plenty of coarsely ground black pepper and add the chopped parsley.

TO SERVE

Decorate just before serving with the remaining egg, quartered. Eat hot and serve the cream and parsley sauce separately, as kedgeree can be rather dry. This is also lovely eaten cold.

Trout Fried in Oatmeal

'When we came back to the Little Shiel, after walking for an hour, we had tea. Brown had caught some excellent trout and cooked them with oatmeal, which the dear Empress liked extremely, and said would be her dinner.'

Queen Victoria LEAVES FROM A JOURNAL OF OUR LIFE IN THE HIGHLANDS 1848–61; on this occasion the Empress Eugenie was visiting Balmoral.

Herrings in oatmeal are made in exactly the same manner, and are much better than plain fried herrings as the oatmeal absorbs some of the fat from these rather oily but deliciously flavoured fish. You can also cook mackerel in this way.

Serves 2

2 very fresh trout, boned (see below)

2 handfuls medium oatmeal

1 oz (25 g) butter

1 tbsp oil

salt

Ask the fishmonger to bone the trout through the back, so that they look like kippers. Remove the slime from the skin side with kitchen paper and sprinkle both sides with oatmeal, pressing it in well to form an even coating.

Heat the butter and oil in a frying pan and fry the trout for 4–5 minutes on each side over a moderate heat. Sprinkle with salt about half-way through the cooking. Turn them carefully so they do not break up and fry until cooked through and a good crisp hazelnut colour on each side.

TO SERVE

Serve at once with new potatoes and buttermilk or butter.

Smoked Trout Mousse

The caterers' trick is to cover everything with a thick layer of aspic which won't dissolve in a hot crowded room, so aspic has now got rather a bad name. But if it is properly made and used with a light hand, it can be rather pretty, fresh and sparkling.

Serves 4–6

a 10 oz (300 g) smoked trout

1½ tsp powdered gelatine (or enough aspic to set ½ pint/300 ml)

¼ pint (150 ml) double cream

salt

cayenne pepper

few drops of lemon juice

1 tsp tarragon vinegar

2 egg whites

few leaves of fresh tarragon, flat parsley or chervil

Skin, bone and flake the trout. Dissolve the gelatine or aspic in 2½ fl oz (60 ml) very hot water. Purée the smoked trout in a liquidiser or food processor and mix the purée with the liquid gelatine or aspic.

Whip the cream lightly and mix into the fish mixture, taste for seasoning and add salt, cayenne, lemon juice and tarragon vinegar. Adjust the flavours to suit your palate, but make it fairly strong.

Whisk the egg whites until firm and fold them into the mixture. Transfer it to a china dish.

Cover with the thinnest possible layer of aspic and chill until it is tacky. Then decorate by arranging a garland of herbs round the edge; chill again. When they are well set, finish with another layer of aspic. Chill again and serve with cucumber salad.

ALTERNATIVE
This can be used another way: divide the mixture between eight small slices of smoked salmon or smoked sturgeon and fold them into rolls. Allow to set, and give each person two rolls and a quarter of a lemon. You can decorate the plates with a few leaves of curly endive.

Fly fishing on the River Wharfe, North Yorkshire

Grilled Dover Sole

1 Dover sole per person

softened butter

salt and freshly ground pepper

Have the fish skinned, trimmed and cleaned.

Heat the grill until it glows before you start to grill the fish. Line the grill pan with buttered kitchen foil. Spread butter over one side of the fish and season with salt and pepper. Grill exactly like a piece of toast, for 4 minutes, until golden brown; then turn the fish over and butter and season the other side. Put them back under the grill and cook for 4 minutes more until golden brown and just cooked through.

Sole vary in thickness and obviously thin ones take less time than thick ones. To test for doneness, look at the head end of the fish and see if it is dry and not pink or red in colour.

TO SERVE
Serve very plain with quartered lemons and fried potatoes, or possibly with tartare sauce and small new potatoes.

ALTERNATIVES
This recipe is also perfect for lemon sole, large plaice, dabs, etc.

Fried Dover Sole

'The best liquor to fry Fish in, is to take Butter and Salet Oyl first well clarified together. This hath not the unsavoury taste of Oyl alone nor the blackness of Butter alone. It fryeth Fish crisp, yellow and well tasted.'
Sir Kenelm Digby THE CLOSET OF SIR KENELM DIGBY KNIGHT, OPENED 1669

1 fine Dover sole per person, skinned by the fishmonger, head removed and trimmed

½ oz (15 g) butter per fish

1 tsp sunflower oil per fish

dusting of flour

salt

1 lemon

Unless you have a heroic-sized frying pan it is best to do fried sole when there are only two or three people to cook for, as they take up a lot of room in the pan, and are best eaten the minute they are cooked.

Heat the butter and oil in a large frying pan, dust the fish with plenty of flour and some salt and as the butter foams and then turns nut-brown, slide them into the pan. Fry for 4 minutes on each side over a brisk heat but without letting the butter become darker than a hazelnut brown. Four minutes each side is fine for an ordinary fish, allow 5 for a large, well-covered one. Remove with a fish-slice, draining off the butter and oil, and serve at once with butter and quartered lemons. Sole should be just cooked through but very firm.

Plaice and lemon sole can be cooked in exactly the same way.

Fishing boats at Oban, Argyllshire

Red Mullet with Anchovies

If you can get fresh red mullet you can cook their livers with the anchovies; they are considered to be very good.

Serves 4

4 red mullet, about 8 oz (225 g) each, or 8 small ones, cleaned

2 oz (50 g) tin anchovies in oil

½ oz (15 g) butter

1 tbsp sunflower or arachide oil

salt

1 lemon, cut in quarters

Scrape the mullet well with the back of a knife to remove all the scales. Rinse them well and dry.

Heat the butter and oil in a frying pan and fry the mullet for about 4–5 minutes on each side. Sprinkle with salt, transfer to a heated dish and keep hot.

Put the anchovies in the frying pan and fry them until they have almost dissolved. Draw them to one side of the pan, draining off the oil, and put them in two mounds, one at each end of the dish with the fried mullet.

TO SERVE

Give each person a little mound of anchovies, a red mullet and quarter of a lemon. Serve with new potatoes, cooked in their skins, and perhaps some mushrooms sliced, fried in butter and oil and very heavily seasoned with coarse black pepper.

Fresh fish for sale, Barnstaple, North Devon

Turbot with Shrimp Sauce

As far as the British are concerned, the sauce for turbot, brill or halibut — those delicious white-fleshed, thick, flat fish — needs to be plain. In good traditional kitchens, the simple white or béchamel sauce is beautifully made and has a pure flavour which is enhanced by one simple ingredient. Often it is a humble handful of chopped parsley — parsley sauce is delicious with turbot. For a slightly more lavish occasion, it might be oyster sauce, or lobster sauce, or shrimp sauce.

It has become fashionable to think that sauces must be made without flour — but the French sauces, based on quantities of reduced cream and butter, are exceedingly rich, while our plain sauces cause no distress to the liver, are as good as they ever were and should not be neglected.

Serves 4

4 turbot steaks (or halibut or brill), weighing 8 oz (225 g) each

salt

¾ pint (425 ml) milk

FOR THE SAUCE

½ pint (300 ml) milk

1 onion

1 bayleaf

8 black peppercorns

12 oz (350 g) prawns or shrimps in shells

1 oz (25 g) butter

1 oz (25 g) flour

1–2 tbsp cream

SAUCE

Heat the milk with the onion, bayleaf and peppercorns, and let it infuse for 10 minutes. Shell the prawns and cook the shells gently in this milk for 10 minutes, then strain the liquid into a bowl, mashing the shells well with a wooden spoon. Melt the butter in a small saucepan and stir in the flour. Let it cook for 2–3 minutes then remove from the heat. Add the strained milk gradually to the butter and flour roux, stirring until it is smooth after each addition.

Let the sauce cook gently for about 5–10 minutes. Then add 1–2 tbsp cream and whisk it thoroughly with a birch or stainless steel whisk; taste for seasoning, add the shellfish and heat through.

COOKING THE FISH

Bring about 4 pints (2.2 litres) well-salted water to the boil, add the milk and when it returns to simmering point turn the heat down until it is barely moving (175°F, 80°C). Slide in the turbot, let it poach very gently for 15–18 minutes depending on the thickness of the steaks, and then remove to a heated serving dish.

TO SERVE

A few boiled new potatoes go well with this poached fish, and the accompanying shrimp sauce should be very hot.

A boat basket, in use in the early twentieth century, probably from Southport, Lancashire

Scalloped Oysters in their Shells

'... Miss Barker had ordered ... all sorts of good things for supper — scalloped oysters, potted lobsters, jelly, a dish called "little Cupids" (which was in great favour with the Cranford ladies, though too expensive to be given — except on solemn and state occasions — macaroons sopped in brandy, I should have called it if I had not known its more refined and classical name). In short, we were evidently to be feasted with all that was sweetest and best ...'
Mrs Gaskell CRANFORD 1853

Scalloped oysters certainly are sweetest and best; even people who do not like raw ones like these. I leave the oysters in their half-shells because they look so ravishingly pretty, whereas six oysters on a plate without their shells are very disappointing little things.

Oysters from a small oyster farm at Orford, Suffolk

Serves 4

1½ oz (40 g) butter
1½ oz (40 g) fresh breadcrumbs
24 oysters
6 tbsp double cream
1 tsp freshly squeezed lemon juice
plenty of cayenne pepper

Melt the butter and fry the breadcrumbs until golden and crisp. Shell the oysters (see below), keeping the deep halves of the shells, and enough liquid just to cover the oysters in a small pan. Pick out all the stray bits of shell and bring the oysters to a simmer in their liquid. Remove them at once from the heat and strain them, keeping the liquid for the sauce. (Oysters shrink alarmingly if cooked for more than a few seconds.) Wash the half shells and put an oyster in each.

Make a sauce with the cream, 4 tbsp strained oyster liquor, lemon juice and quite a lot of cayenne pepper. Let it simmer until it has reduced to a light but creamy texture.

Taste it for seasoning — it probably will not need salt — and pour some of this sauce over each oyster. Sprinkle the oyster itself with fried crumbs and heat through quickly under the grill or in the oven. Serve at once, with bread to mop up the juices.

A NOTE ON OPENING OYSTERS

Get the fishmonger to open them and carry them home in a container inside an insulated bag, the sort that you use for picnics. Cook them as soon as you get home. They can then be sprinkled with breadcrumbs and reheated at the last minute, but should be eaten within a few hours.

Alternatively, provide yourself with an oyster knife, teatowels and a wide shallow dish. Wrap your left hand in a teatowel, hold an oyster in the palm of that hand, deep shell downwards and with the hinge towards you. Insert the blade of the oyster-knife into the side of the hinge, finding a tiny hole or crevice — not always easy — and twist it; for Portuguese oysters, insert the knife blade at the end opposite the hinge. Cut the oyster off and turn it over so that you see the pretty plump side.

Scallops with Fried Breadcrumbs

The surest way to ruin scallops is to overcook them, they should be very succulent and tender.

Serves 4

12 fresh scallops

1 oz (25 g) butter

4 tbsp olive oil

1½ oz (40 g) fresh white breadcrumbs

salt and freshly ground pepper

1 lemon

Clean and wash the scallops and put them to drain and dry in a colander.

Heat half the butter and oil in a small frying pan and fry the breadcrumbs, moving them about all the time to prevent them burning, until they are a good even brown and quite crisp.

Heat the remaining oil and butter in a second pan. When it is very hot, put in the scallops, then turn down the heat a little and let them cook and glaze to a glossy brown over a moderate heat for about 2 minutes on each side — but make sure they keep frying and don't start cooking in their own juices.

Season with salt and pepper, throw the breadcrumbs over the scallops and cook for ½ minute more.

TO SERVE
Serve at once, well sprinkled with the crumbs, with a quarter of a lemon on each plate.

Dublin Lawyer

This recipe is, as it sounds, Irish and comes from Theodora Fitzgibbon's book *Irish Traditional Food*. I use ordinary whisky when I make it; it is still sensationally good.

Serves 2

1 fresh cooked lobster weighing 1½ lb (675 g)

2 oz (50 g) butter

2–3 tbsp Irish whiskey (or ordinary whisky)

¼ pint (150 ml) double cream

salt

cayenne pepper

Cut the lobster in half and remove the meat from the claws and shells. When cracking the claws it helps to cover them with a cloth before hitting them with a rolling pin, to stop the shell splinters flying all over the kitchen. Keep the body shells to serve the lobster in, and don't try to remove the small legs or the interior casing of the head. Leave the greenish tomalley in place.

Cut the lobster meat into ¾ inch (2 cm) chunks and put it in a small pan with the butter. Heat gently, turning the pieces until well coated. Heat the whiskey, light it and pour it over the lobster. When the flames die down remove the pieces of lobster with a slotted spoon and add the cream to the pan. Mix it with the pan juices and add seasoning. Boil until it is reduced to a rich and creamy sauce, about 3 minutes. Put the lobster back into the sauce, turning it over to heat it through, then pile into the shells and serve very hot.

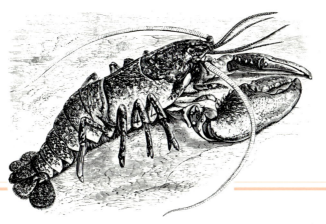

Crabs and traditional pots, made by hand from hazel and willow, on the beach at Beer, South Devon

Dressed Crab

Fresh crab has a much more luscious texture than frozen and far more flavour, so the performance needed to get it all out of its shell is more than worth it. We consider it is quite as good as lobster, if not better. Always choose a heavy one; light crabs tend to be dry and wasted inside.

A 2 lb (900 g) crab serves 1;
a 3–4 lb (1.3–1.8 kg) crab serves 2

Ask the fishmonger to loosen the body of the crab from the shell or carapace for you, so he can see it is a good fleshy crab, and to remove the gills which are also known as 'deadman's fingers' and are not edible.

With a wood mallet, hammer or a rolling pin, a skewer and a large wooden chopping board at the ready, open up the crab, pulling the slender legs and the lower body away from the top shell. Take all the brown meat from around the inside of the top shell and a few teaspoons more from the centre of the crab's body. Put it into a bowl, season lightly with fresh black or cayenne pepper and a few drops of lemon juice and mash it with a fork until it is smooth. Taste and add salt, if it is needed.

Now crack the large claws and remove the white meat, flaking it into a separate bowl. Cut the body into 3 pieces with a large heavy knife and pick out the meat from all the little shell cavities with a skewer, taking care not to get flakes of shell into the bowl. On a large crab you can also break the long thin claws with your hands and extract the meat from these. Mix the white meat with a couple of tablespoons of mayonnaise, if liked.

Arrange the small crisp inner leaves of a Cos lettuce or endive all around a deep dish and pile the white meat in a ring around the edges. Put the brown meat in the centre.

TO SERVE
Serve with slices of brown bread and butter, quarters of lemon and a bowl of mayonnaise for those who like a richer dressed crab.

Fish Pie with Prawns

'The cook should be well acquainted with the signs of freshness and good condition in fish, as they are most unwholesome articles of food when stale, and many of them are also dangerous eating when they are out of season. The eyes should always be bright, the gills of a fine clear red, the body stiff, the flesh firm, yet elastic to the touch, and the smell not disagreeable.'

Eliza Acton MODERN COOKERY FOR PRIVATE
FAMILIES 1845

Nobody has bettered Eliza Acton's description of really fresh fish. Even for fish pie, the fresher the fish the better the results. This pie is good-tempered, reheats wonderfully and can be kept waiting. It can be made the day before and also freezes quite successfully.

Serves 6

1½ lb (675 g) fresh haddock or cod fillets

1 lb (450 g) Finnan haddock on the bone or 12 oz (350 g) smoked haddock fillets

¾ pint (425 ml) milk

1½ oz (40 g) butter

12 oz (350 g) prawns in their shells

1 bayleaf

6 peppercorns

1½ oz (40 g) flour

salt

1 small tsp white wine vinegar

2 tbsp single or double cream

½ tsp or more freshly ground black pepper

mashed potatoes made with 1½ lb (675 g) potatoes, milk and butter

Preheat the oven to 350°F (180°C, Gas 4). Put the fillets of fish and smoked haddock in an ovenproof dish with the milk. Dot with ½ oz (15 g) butter and cook in the oven for 20 minutes. Skin the fish, remove the bones and keep it on one side.

Shell the prawns (reserving the shells), and put them with the fish.

Heat the milk in which the fish was cooked, together with the prawn shells, bayleaf and peppercorns. Let it infuse over a very low heat for at least 10 minutes.

Melt the remaining 1 oz (25 g) butter in a medium-sized pan, stir in the flour and let it cook for a minute. Then remove from the heat and add the strained milk. Make a nice thick, smooth sauce, then season it carefully with salt, wine vinegar and cream, and masses of black pepper. The flavour of this sauce is most important and mustn't be bland. Stir in the fish and prawns and transfer the mixture to a 10 inch (25 cm) oval pie dish. Cover with well-seasoned mashed potato, dot with butter and cook in the oven at 400°F (200°C, Gas 6) until the top is nicely browned. Serve very hot.

Fish Pie

Serves 4

12 oz (350 g) smoked haddock fillet

3 hard-boiled eggs

¼ pint (150 ml) milk

1 bayleaf

1½ oz (40 g) butter

1 oz (25 g) flour

1 tsp white wine vinegar

3–4 tbsps chopped fresh parsley

salt and freshly ground pepper

mashed potatoes made with 3–4 good-sized
   potatoes (about 1 lb/450 g), milk and butter

Preheat the oven to 325°F (170°C, Gas 3).
   Put the fish in a dish with the milk and ¼ pint
(150 ml) water, a bayleaf and ½ oz (15 g) butter.
Cook in the oven for 15–20 minutes. When it is
done, strain off the liquid and allow the fish to cool
so that you can skin, bone and flake it.
   Melt the remaining 1 oz (25 g) butter in a
medium-sized pan, stir in the flour and let it cook
for a minute. Then remove from the heat and add
the vinegar and some of the liquid from the fish.
Return the pan to the heat and stir until you have a
fairly thick smooth sauce, adding more of the fish
liquid if necessary. Add no salt yet.
   Mix together the sauce, fish, shelled sliced
hard-boiled eggs and the chopped parsley. Taste
and add salt if it is needed. Put the mixture into a
pie dish. Carefully cover with a rough layer of
well-seasoned mashed potato, dot the top with
butter and brown the pie in a hot oven, 400–425°F
(200–220°C, Gas 6–7), for at least 20 minutes.

VARIATION
Instead of eggs you could add scallops poached in
the same liquid as the fish and cut in quarters, or
crisp, white, button mushrooms lightly sautéed in
butter. You can also add cream for a richer result.

Traditional Fish and Chips

*'This was a good dinner to be sure; but it was not a
dinner to ask a man to.'*
James Boswell THE LIFE OF SAMUEL JOHNSON
1791

In other words, this is a homely, family sort of food;
it is difficult to entertain friends while standing over
a sizzling pan of chips. Fish and chips and the
British have long been inseparable — we even insist
on them in the seaports of the Mediterranean,
where they do, I believe, have their own ideas about
cooking fish. But in spite of the story that they can
only be eaten out of newspapers and standing up,
they are in fact very fine food, particularly when
home made. Fresh haddock is the best fish to use,
but you can also use cod, plaice or hake.
   Deep fat frying has been made very much easier
recently by the invention of domestic deep fat frying
machines with thermostats. If you have the oil at the
right temperatures, the fish and the chips will each
be perfectly cooked when they are just the right
shade of golden brown.

Serves 6

7 oz (200 g) self-raising flour

1 tsp salt

½ tsp baking powder

3 large haddock fillets, about 10 oz (300 g) each

vegetable oil for frying

First get the chips ready (see right), then make the
batter. Mix the flour, salt and baking powder and
gradually beat in up to ½ pint (300 ml) water to make
a thick, rather white batter. Allow to stand for at
least an hour, then beat again. Skin the haddock
fillets and cut them in half.
   Heat the vegetable oil in a deep-frying pan with a
basket until it reaches 350–375°F (180–190°C). Dip
the pieces of fish first in flour and then in the batter,
coating them well but not too thickly.
   Deep fry to a crisp golden brown. Drain on
kitchen paper. Keep hot in the oven with the door
slightly open, while you fry the chips.

Bideford Bay, North Devon

THE CHIPS
$2\frac{1}{2}$–3 lb (1.1–1.3 kg) potatoes (Maris Piper are supposed to be the best)

Peel the potatoes and cut into chips of the size you like. If you want to, you can cut the two round ends off each potato before cutting them, so that you have square ended chips. Put them in a bowl of cold water, and leave them there until just before you are ready to start frying the fish. Then drain and dry them in a cloth. After frying the fish heat the oil in the deep-frying pan to 390–400°F (about 200°C).

Lower the chips, a few at a time, into the hot fat and fry in batches, to a golden brown. Drain well, lay out on a baking tin lined with kitchen paper, sprinkle with salt and keep hot in the oven.

Serve the fish and chips with lemon wedges.

Fried Cod's Roe

Instead of being salted and smoked, the cod's roe is freshly boiled by the fishmonger and sold cooked and ready to fry. Simply slice it thickly, dust with flour and fry in butter or bacon fat. It is delicious with fried bacon.

A more formal way of serving it is to place the fried cod's roe on rounds of fried bread or toast and season with cayenne pepper. Serve as a first course or a light supper, or, as it used to be eaten, as a savoury after a good dinner.

An alternative is to dip the slices first in flour and then in beaten eggs before frying.

Breakfast Kedgeree

This is a very good breakfast kedgeree; it can be kept hot while people wander downstairs for a weekend perusal of the newspapers in their dressing-gowns, and it reheats well for anybody who has been out walking or gardening early, or stayed out late the night before.

Serves 4

1 lb (450 g) smoked haddock fillet

½ pint (300 ml) milk

1 strip lemon rind

1 bayleaf

2½ oz (65 g) butter

3 hard-boiled eggs

6 oz (175 g) Basmati rice

salt

cayenne pepper

Preheat the oven to 375°F (190°C, Gas 5).

Cook the haddock in a buttered roasting tin with the milk and ¼ pint (150 ml) water, lemon rind, bayleaf and ½ oz (15 g) butter for 15 minutes. Allow to cool. Chop the hard-boiled eggs.

Cook the rice very lightly, either in salted water or, better, in the cooking liquid from the fish. Mix together the rice, which should be well-drained or have absorbed all its liquid, according to the method of cooking, with the chopped eggs. Flake the haddock and stir it in. Add 2 oz (50 g) butter and heat through, tossing lightly with a fork. Sprinkle well with cayenne, fork the kedgeree through once more and serve very hot.

VARIATION

To turn this into a richer, supper dish, cook the fish in all milk, instead of milk and water. Then use the fishy milk, with half the butter, 1 oz (25 g) flour and 1 tsp curry powder, to make a creamy sauce. Pour the sauce into the kedgeree and heat it right through until it bubbles, then serve at once.

Omelette Arnold Bennett

You can use haddock fillets for this, but the flavour is less good if they are coloured golden-yellow with dye, and are not the natural pale gold colour of a properly cured and smoked haddock on the bone.

Serves 4

2 whole Finnan haddock (smoked haddock) weighing 12 oz (350 g) each, or 1 weighing 1½ lb (675 g)

½ pint (300 ml) milk

water

1 oz (25 g) butter

6 eggs

1½–2 oz (40–50 g) finely grated cheese — a mixture of Parmesan, Gruyère and Cheddar is ideal

¼ pint (150 ml) double cream

salt

Preheat the oven to 325°F (170°C, Gas 3).

Put the haddock face downwards in a small roasting tin with the milk and a little water. Dot with a few nuts of the butter and cook in the oven for 15–20 minutes, until just cooked through. Allow the fish to become cool enough to handle and remove all the bones and the skin. Flake the fish into a bowl.

Beat the eggs and stir them into the haddock, together with all but a tablespoon or so of the cheese. Taste the mixture and add a little salt if necessary. Whip the cream and heat the grill.

Heat a tablespoon of butter in a frying pan and, when it starts to brown, pour in the egg mixture. Cook for a few minutes and move the mixture around with a spatula, so that it does not burn. When the bottom is set, put the frying pan under the grill until the top is all but set. Then spread the cream over the top, sprinkle with the rest of the grated cheese and glaze to a beautiful flecked golden brown under the grill.

TO SERVE

Serve it hot, cut in wedges like a cake. I find this omelette is also delicious cold.

Creamed Smokies

The Jersey cream gives this dish a rich yellow colour that I like. Ordinary double cream is quite suitable, though rather pallid.

Serves 6

1½ lb (675 g) smokies (or smoked haddock) on the bone

3 hard-boiled eggs

8 fl oz (225 ml) double Jersey cream

cayenne pepper

IF USING SMOKED HADDOCK

Preheat the oven to 325°F (170°C, Gas 3). Pour boiling water over the haddocks in a roasting tin. Put them into the heated oven and cook until just done, 15–20 minutes, when a milky liquid will start to emerge between the flakes of fish. Drain and flake the fish when it is cool enough, removing all the skin and bones.

IF USING ARBROATH SMOKIES

These are already cooked — skin, bone and flake carefully.

Peel the hard-boiled eggs and cut them in half lengthwise, then slice fairly thinly. Heat the cream, sprinkle generously with cayenne and let it boil gently until thickened somewhat. Carefully transfer the haddock and eggs to the cream and fold them in gently. Heat through.

TO SERVE

Puff pastry cheese straws (page 29) are good with this, or if you like you can decorate it with fresh, juicy, peeled prawns, previously heated through in a tablespoon or two of fresh cream, but I like it plain.

Another variation is to use curry powder instead of cayenne, in which case leave the curry powder out of the cheese straws.

Salmon and herrings being smoked over oakwood, Orford, Suffolk

Sheep in the shade of May trees, Addisford, North Devon

MEAT, POULTRY AND GAME

Until the Industrial Revolution, meat, together with bread, cheese and ale, was the preferred diet of everyone in Britain; and many cottagers kept a pig who was respectfully called 'the gentleman that pays the rent'. Beef was mostly for gentry and pork, ham and boiled bacon were for the cottagers: this was supplanted in sheep-rearing areas by mutton. Veal was a little-known delicacy, but poultry was everybody's favourite: the art of rearing poultry was highly skilled and complicated and the results were, as we now realise, much better flavoured than today's factory-farmed, pellet-fed poultry.

Game, after the middle ages, was not for the poor, who could face imprisonment or even worse for poaching. Rabbits they were allowed to take, but game belonged to the land owner himself and in England and Scotland it usually still does (although deer poaching in the Scottish Highlands is secretly a rather skilled and respected trade, the poachers often using crossbows, which have the advantage of being silent). In England, of course, we take a frightfully poor view of this sort of thing, whereas the Irish are often portrayed as born poachers who love every minute of it, as anyone who has read The Experiences of an Irish R.M. *(by Somerville and Ross) will know. However it finds its way to you, British game is second to none and is something to cheer your table in autumn and winter.*

In the kitchen at Great Dixter, East Sussex

Roasting Meat

'...four Spits ... carry round each five or six pieces of Butcher's Meat, Beef, Mutton, Veal, Pork and Lamb; you have what Quality you please cut off, fat, lean, much or little done; with this, a little salt and Mustard upon the Side of a Plate, a Bottle of Beer and a Roll; and there is your whole Feast.'
Henri Misson de Valbourg, a French cleric
H. MISSON'S MEMOIRS AND OBSERVATIONS IN HIS TRAVELS OVER ENGLAND 1690

Although it is usual to give a table for roasting meat, this doesn't always work exactly right. First of all everyone's oven is different; an Aga cooks differently from a conventional oven at the same temperature, and the newest fan ovens cook differently again. Then each piece of meat you buy is an individual and unique piece, differing in shape, size, thickness of fat, weight of bone, age and moisture content from the one you bought last week. A thick piece of meat will take longer to roast than a thin roll, but a rolled, boned loin of pork is quite dense, and so will take as long or longer than a much chunkier looking loin on the bone. After a while you will start adjusting by 5 or 10 minutes according to the look of a joint; a light, slender-looking leg of lamb will need a good 20 minutes less than a short, plump one.

Even more important, people like their meat cooked in different ways. Some people like rare beef and well done lamb. Some love everything except pork to have a decidedly rose-pink centre and others like pork really overcooked to be on the safe side, although this is not necessary. Some people like long slow roasting and others, especially chefs, like to do everything at the highest temperature and as fast as possible, and then to let it relax and recover afterwards. So any times given are for a general guide, rather than hard and fast rules.

'Premier' roaster: bakeware from *The Ironmonger* 28 June 1913

The Best Way to Roast Beef

'Sir, my brain is obfuscated after the perusal of this heterogeneous conglomeration of bastard English ill-spelt, and a foreign tongue. I prithe bid thy knaves bring me a dish of hogs pudding a slice or two from one upper cut of a well-roasted sirloin, and two apple dumplings.'
Samuel Johnson after perusing a French menu

The best way to achieve a really well-roasted sirloin or rib of roast beef is to buy the very best beef from a good butcher, one who hangs his meat. This makes a difference; beef that hasn't been hung properly is not rewarding as it hasn't had time to develop flavour and succulence.

The art of roasting is not learned by reading a recipe, but by practice. Even now, after twenty years or more of roasting meat, I can still get some nasty surprises.

Roughly speaking, a rare 6 lb (2.6 kg) rib or sirloin of beef on the bone will take 1½ hours to cook (i.e. 15 minutes per lb or 450 g) at 375°F (190°C, Gas 5), and will need half an hour's rest at the end before carving, to give it time to relax. Rest it in a warm place, and keep it covered with an old-fashioned meat cover or a loose tent of kitchen foil.

Smear the meat with butter and oil and sprinkle it with salt before you put it in the oven — some people like to put it on a small rack in the roasting tin. Baste and turn it every 20 minutes or so, while it cooks. Keep an eye on it to see it is progressing well — if not you can turn the oven up or down a little — this can depend on what else is in the oven with the beef. It doesn't roast as quickly in a very steamy oven, or if there are lots of potatoes around it, and other things taking up the heat.

Allow 6 lb (2.6 kg) beef on the bone for 10 people. Allow 4½–5 lb (2–2.2 kg) boned and rolled beef for 10 people. Rare cold beef is always useful afterwards, whereas if you run out of meat, or have to be ungenerous with it, you will feel most put out.

Carving is much easier if the joint has been boned and rolled. If not, a prime sirloin of beef will have two sides to it, the top or sirloin and the undercut or fillet. Each person should get some of each.

Inexperienced carvers should remove the meat from the bone before attempting to slice it up. The ends will be for people who like it better done, the middle for those who like it rare.

Yorkshire Pudding

At one time Yorkshire pudding, the traditional English accompaniment to roast beef, was always served before the beef to fill the family and take the edge off their appetites, so that a small joint of beef would go round large numbers of children, grannies and aunts. Nowadays, we serve it with the beef, together with roast potatoes, a green vegetable and a simple gravy made from the dripping from the meat.

Make the batter 1 hour before you start to cook the pudding. Using an extra egg gives the pudding a very good rise, but perhaps a less succulent texture.

Serves 6

4 oz (100 g) plain flour

¼ pint (150 ml) milk and water, mixed

1 or 2 eggs, beaten

good pinch of salt

3 tbsp dripping

Put the flour in a bowl, gradually add the milk and water and the beaten egg or eggs, stirring all the time with a wooden spoon until the batter is smooth. Add a pinch of salt, beat well and allow the batter to stand for 1 hour.

Heat the dripping in a small roasting tin in a hot oven (425°F, 220°C, Gas 7), pour the batter into the hot fat and bake at the top of the oven over the meat for 30 minutes until the pudding is well risen and brown.

Grilled Beefsteak and Horseradish

'One thing is certain when we do find English cookery correctly prepared: it is the best and wholesomest in the world, because it is the most simple and retains the delicious flavour of food noted for its excellence; a failure cannot be camouflaged.'
Florence White GOOD THINGS IN ENGLAND 1932

One of our great traditional foods was meat, well-hung steak and chops grilled over or in front of a lovely bright fire — often a bed of coals — and served red hot with a good grill sauce. These sauces tended to be hot too, containing mustard, Worcestershire sauce, cayenne and horseradish, or perhaps sharp pickles, capers and cucumbers. This kind of food was particularly enjoyed earlier in the century by business men, in the cosy steamy atmosphere of the many thriving chop-houses, grill rooms and inns, that provided them with an alternative to domesticity.

The horseradish sauce is much better if made with freshly grated horseradish root, although your eyes will stream whilst you grate it. You can sometimes buy fresh horseradish or find the roots growing — they thrive in allotments, on railway embankments and in old vegetable gardens. Otherwise you can buy it ready grated in jars.

8 oz (225 g) rump or sirloin steak per person (fillet steak is not tasty enough for this)

softened butter or oil

salt and pepper

HORSERADISH SAUCE

2 tbsp grated horseradish, fresh or preserved

1 tbsp white wine vinegar

a little English mustard

pinch salt

pinch sugar

4 tbsp double cream

a little cayenne pepper

Herding cattle at Hollocombe, North Devon

FOR THE SAUCE
Mix all the ingredients together in a bowl and taste a little to see if the balance of flavours is right. Keep at room temperature and use the same day.

FOR THE BEEFSTEAK
Heat the grill so that it is really glowing before you start to cook. Rub the steak all over with softened butter or vegetable oil. Put it close to the grill at first and allow it to become very frizzled on the outsides, then move it a little further from the heat, sprinkle with salt and pepper and cook a few more minutes, turning it once. You can tell how well it is done by pressing it with your finger. A 'blue' steak will feel soft and yielding, 'rare' will be yielding but not too soft and wobbly, while a resilient or bouncy texture means the steak is well done right through.

TO SERVE
Serve a beautifully grilled steak straight from the grill on a hot plate with the horseradish sauce, fried potatoes and a salad.

Sirloin, from *Good Plain Cookery* by Mary Hooper, 1882

Steak and Kidney Pudding

'This is a national English dish par excellence,' Countess Morphy says of Steak and Kidney Pie in her book of *English Recipes*, but I think it is even truer of Steak and Kidney Pudding, an unforgettable treat.

Serves 6

2 lb (900 g) beef, including chuck steak or other juicy stewing steak, and a piece of skirt

8 oz (225 g) ox kidney

1 oz (25 g) seasoned flour

2 oz (50 g) button mushrooms, cleaned and trimmed (optional)

1 tbsp Worcestershire sauce

dash of Tabasco sauce

1 tbsp mushroom ketchup (optional)

salt and coarsely ground black pepper

beef stock or water

FOR THE SUET CRUST

4 oz (100 g) shredded suet

8 oz (225 g) self-raising flour

salt

PASTRY

Mix the suet, flour and salt in a bowl and then add just enough cold water to bind it — don't add too much at first, this mixture should be light and spongy, not wet. Roll it out, keeping back about a quarter for the lid, and line a buttered 2 pint (1.1 litre) pudding basin.

FILLING

Trim the meat of fat and sinews and cut it into cubes. Cut the kidney into pieces the size of small walnuts. Roll the beef and kidney in seasoned flour, mix with the mushrooms and put into the basin. Mix the Worcestershire sauce, Tabasco and mushroom ketchup and pour it in, then add enough well-seasoned beef stock or water to come two-thirds to three-quarters of the way up the sides. Use plenty of pepper in the seasoning. Moisten the top edge of the crust.

Roll out the remaining pastry to make a lid. Cover the pudding, press firmly to seal, then trim and roll the edges over inwards, pressing lightly.

Pleat a piece of foil and cover the top of the pudding loosely with it, tying it round under the rim of the basin with string. Make a handle by passing the string across the top two or three times — not too tightly as the pudding must have room to expand. Lower into a large pan of boiling water with a close-fitting lid; the water should come two-thirds of the way up the basin, and must be topped up as it boils away. If the pudding leaks a bit, don't worry. Boil, covered, for 4–5 hours.

Lift the pudding out of the pan and remove the foil. Wrap the basin in a clean white napkin, with the top crust showing fluffy and slightly browned from its collar of white linen. If the crust has come in contact with water, it may be pale and glistening; it will still be delicious to eat.

TO SERVE

Serve the fragrant pudding with a green vegetable such as spring greens. A good claret is best with steak and kidney pudding.

Steak and Kidney Pie

'One of the few plants I found in the derelict garden when we came to live here was a sweet bay-tree. It flourishes just outside the kitchen door, and I doubt whether there is a day of the year when we do not pull one leaf, at least, for use in cooking.'
Constance Spry COME INTO THE GARDEN COOK 1942

Serves 6

2½ lb (1.1 kg) chuck steak or other good braising steak

10 oz (350 g) ox kidney

2 onions

2 tbsp lard or vegetable oil

1 oz (25 g) flour

¼ pint (150 ml) red wine

1 pint (550 ml) beef stock

dash Worcestershire sauce

1 tsp mushroom ketchup (optional)

bunch of herbs — thyme, bay and parsley

salt and freshly ground black pepper

12 oz (350 g) rough puff pastry, made from 6 oz/175 g flour (see page 138)

1 egg yolk, for glazing

Preheat the oven to 325°F (170°C, Gas 3). Cut the beef into 1½ inch (4 cm) pieces — keep them chunky and rather large so they do not lose their succulence. Trim off all the fat and sinew. Core the kidney and cut into walnut-sized pieces. Peel and slice the onions, not too thinly.

Heat the lard or vegetable oil in a casserole, and when it starts to smoke, fry the beef and kidney a few pieces at a time, so that it is browned on all sides. Remove the pieces to a dish as they brown. When all the meat is done, brown the onions in the same fat.

Return the meat to the casserole and sprinkle on the flour. Let it brown, then add the red wine and beef stock, stirring to incorporate the flour and deglaze the bottom of the casserole. Add the Worcestershire sauce, mushroom ketchup and the herbs and seasonings and bring to a slow simmer on the top of the stove. Then cover the casserole and transfer to the low oven to simmer for 1½–2 hours — test to see if it is done after 1½ hours. Remove from the oven, take out the herbs and allow to cool. Taste and adjust the seasoning if necessary.

Transfer the meat to a 10 inch (25 cm) pie dish with a pie-funnel in the centre. If you don't think there is enough meat to hold up the crust, put a few peeled and quartered parboiled potatoes on top of the meat and this will do the trick beautifully (and the potatoes will taste delicious). Preheat the oven to 425°F (220°C, Gas 7).

Roll out the pastry. Brush the edge of the pie dish with egg glaze and cut some strips of pastry to fit round the rim of the dish. Brush the strips with glaze, put the remaining pastry on top, trim the edge, scallop it and knock it up with the blade of a knife so that the actual cut edge looks as deep as possible. Make a hole in the centre and cut some leaves from the trimmings to decorate the top. Brush the pie top with egg glaze, place the leaves on top and brush again.

Cook in the very hot oven for 12 minutes, then reduce the temperature to 350°F (180°C, Gas 4) for 30 minutes. Cover lightly with foil if it shows signs of over-browning.

VARIATION

The steak and kidney pie can also have mushrooms in it. Fry them lightly before you fry the onions, keep them on one side and put them into the pie dish with the meat.

TO SERVE

Serve steak and kidney pie with a green vegetable such as Brussels sprouts or lightly cooked buttered cabbage and perhaps some small baked potatoes, or with mashed potatoes and a watercress and chicory salad.

Cattle outside the ruined threshing barn, Beaford Wood, North Devon

Herbed Stew with Dumplings and Pickles

According to my mother, the only herbs used in cooking in her Bradford home were parsley, thyme and sage. A stew would be cooked with plenty of vegetables — carrots, onions and turnips — and with dumplings which were placed on top of the stew and cooked in the upper part of the oven uncovered, so that they became slightly brown.

The usual pickles were pickled red cabbage (page 149), pickled onions (page 150) and pickled walnuts, the latter being the best with beef.

Serves 6

3 lb (1.3 kg) chuck steak
8 oz (225 g) carrots
1 lb (450 g) onions
1 turnip
2–3 tbsp dripping or lard
1 oz (25 g) flour
salt and pepper
thyme and sage — a good sprinkling of each
1 pint (550 ml) beef stock

FOR THE DUMPLINGS

5 oz (150 g) self-raising flour

2 tbsp shredded suet

salt and freshly ground pepper

2 tsp chopped parsley

Preheat the oven to 325°F (170°C, Gas 3).

Cut the meat into cubes, carefully trimming away all the fat and gristle — this makes a world of difference to the final result. Peel and chop the vegetables.

Melt the dripping or lard in an enamelled iron casserole. Sprinkle the meat with the flour and a little salt and pepper and fry, a few pieces at a time, until nicely browned. Transfer the browned pieces of meat to a dish, put the chopped vegetables into the casserole and let them fry a little. Then return the meat and its juices, together with stock, the herbs and a good seasoning of salt and pepper. Bring to the boil, scraping the sediment from the bottom of the casserole, and then cover and transfer to the oven. Leave to cook for $1\frac{1}{2}$–$1\frac{3}{4}$ hours.

Personally, I think this stew cooked in the oven has a richer look and a better, mellower flavour than when cooked on the top of the stove.

DUMPLINGS

Make the dumplings about 45 minutes before the end of the cooking time. Mix the flour, suet, salt, pepper and parsley and add enough water to make a workable dough — it takes about 6–8 tbsp altogether. Shape into walnut-sized dumplings and put these on top of the simmering stew. Leave to cook, uncovered, for 35–40 minutes until nicely browned.

TO SERVE

Serve the stew with its dumplings, and with pickled walnuts, mashed or baked potatoes and perhaps a green salad, which in my grandmother's house would have had lots of malt vinegar and sugar on it, but a more delicious dressing can be found on page 146.

Beef and Cabbage

'When 'midst the frying Pan, in accents savage,
The Beef, so surly, quarrels with the Cabbage.'
Dr Kitchiner THE COOK'S ORACLE 1817

Also known as Bubble and Squeak, this version does not include potatoes, and is as fresh and delicate as you could wish although the recipe itself is at least 150 years old.

It is rather difficult to give exact quantities for a dish like this. However, if you have some rosy-pink roast beef left over, try serving it in the following way. The original recipe insists 'let it remain no longer in the pan than is necessary to make it hot through' — if you ignore this rule, the beef will become tough.

1 green cabbage

8 oz (225 g) or more rare roast beef

$\frac{1}{2}$–1 oz (15–25 g) butter

1–2 tbsp gravy from the roast beef

salt and freshly ground black pepper

dash or two of Worcestershire sauce

Cut away the outer leaves of the cabbage, quarter it, remove the core completely and drop the quarters into plenty of boiling salted water. Boil, uncovered, for 10–15 minutes until the cabbage just turns translucent green, then drain very well and cut up roughly.

Carve the beef into small slices about 2 inches (5 cm) square.

Heat the butter in a frying pan, put in the cabbage and stir it round until it is hot and buttery all the way through. Add the beef, stir briefly, then add the gravy and Worcestershire sauce. Stir round once or twice rapidly over a high heat until the ingredients are all piping hot, season with salt and pepper and serve at once.

Brown Braised Beef with Norfolk Dumplings

The interesting thing about this adaptation of an old recipe called Brown Braise (which called for trimmings of meat rather than a piece of meat itself, and must have been rather like the stew that was offered in British restaurants during the war, where the customers' meat coupons bought them a plate of delicious gravy) is the combination of herbs used. Thyme is predictable, sweet marjoram less so and basil rather a surprise as it is difficult to grow in this country. However, it is an old favourite in Britain and was once an important ingredient in, of all things, mock turtle soup. The herbs were dried, giving a very different flavour to the fresh basil leaves strewn on tomato salad in the summer.

Serves 4–6

2½ lb (1.1 kg) chuck steak

4 large carrots

2 onions and 3 shallots, or 3 onions

small stick of celery

sprinkling of flour

1½ oz (40 g) butter

½ tsp each dried thyme, sweet or knotted marjoram and basil

1 tbsp chopped parsley

4 anchovies, chopped

sprinkling of ground nutmeg or mace

¼ pint (150 ml) white wine

1 pint (550 ml) stock or water

salt and freshly ground pepper

FOR NORFOLK DUMPLINGS

1 egg

¼ pint (150 ml) milk

7–8 oz (200–225 g) self-raising flour

½ tsp salt

1 tbsp chopped parsley

Cut the trimmed beef into ¾ inch (2 cm) cubes. Cut the carrots into ¼ inch (½ cm) rounds and roughly chop the onions and shallots. Flour the meat generously.

Melt 1 oz (25 g) of the butter in a fairly small casserole (this would once have been called a stewpot) and when it starts to brown add the steak, one quarter at a time and fry the pieces not too fast, removing them as they are browned and adding the herbs and anchovies towards the end. Use more butter if necessary.

When all the pieces are browned, return them to the pan, add the vegetables and seasonings and stir everything over a low heat for a few minutes. Then add the wine and stock. Cover the pan and cook for 1½–1¾ hours at a gentle simmer.

TO MAKE THE DUMPLINGS

Beat the egg with the milk, and gradually add to the flour to make a very thick batter. Beat well, adding salt and chopped parsley. Drop a teaspoon of the mixture at a time into boiling water and lift out when they float — after 4–5 minutes. Serve on the stew. Alternatively, you can put teaspoons of the mixture on top of the simmering stew, cover the pan and simmer until they swell and cook through — about 10 minutes.

Bronzed Braised Beef with Guinness

Serves 6

2½ lb (1.1 kg) braising beef, cut in large steaks ¼ inch (½ cm) thick

8 oz (225 g) carrots

8 oz (225 g) small onions

2 shallots

1 pint (550 ml) Guinness

1 bayleaf

2 sprigs parsley

6 peppercorns

1 strip orange rind, pared free of the white pith

salt and freshly ground pepper

1 oz (25 g) butter

1 tbsp oil

a little flour

pinch of sugar

1 tsp vinegar

a little beef stock

THE DAY BEFORE

Trim the meat but keep the pieces whole. Cut the carrots into little sticks about 1½ inches (4 cm) long by ¼ inch (½ cm) across and peel and cut the onions and shallots downwards so that they fall apart into little crescents. Put them into a porcelain dish and pour on the Guinness. Add the bayleaf and parsley, peppercorns and strip of orange rind. Season with a tiny pinch of salt. Put the meat into this marinade and let it marinate overnight. Turn it over once or twice if possible.

NEXT DAY

Drain and dry the steaks. Heat the butter and oil in a wide casserole. Dust the steaks lightly with flour and brown them well on both sides. Remove them to a plate and add the strained vegetables from the marinade (if you prefer you can use fresh). Cook the vegetables over a low heat for a few minutes, stirring them round. Add the marinade and place the beef on top of the vegetables. Add the sugar and vinegar and enough stock to come halfway up the sides of the meat. Season lightly with salt and pepper.

Cover the pan and place over a very low heat — use a heat-diffusing mat if you think the heat is too fierce. Simmer very, very slowly for 1½ hours — the meat is cooked when a skewer pierces it very easily.

You can cook this braised beef in a low oven if you prefer — 325°F (170°C, Gas 3). Serve it with a good dish of mashed potatoes to mop up the delicious gravy, or with baked potatoes and red cabbage.

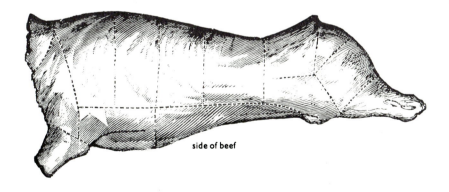

side of beef

Braised Kidneys in Port Wine

These kidneys taste very different to lambs' kidneys fried or grilled in the ordinary way, and make the most wonderful gravy. If you don't have any port you can make a very good dish using red wine.

Serves 4

8–10 lambs' kidneys (fresh if possible)

1 onion

4 oz (100 g) mushrooms

1 oz (25 g) butter

1 tbsp oil

4 sprigs of parsley, chopped

a dusting of flour

$\frac{1}{4}$ pint (150 ml) port

few tbsp good chicken stock

1 tsp coarsely crushed black peppercorns

salt and freshly ground pepper

Skin the kidneys. Peel and chop the onion and trim and slice the mushrooms. Heat the butter and oil in a heavy frying pan and fry the skinned whole kidneys until they are browned all over — 4–5 minutes should be enough. Remove them, allow to cool a little and slice into rounds about $\frac{1}{8}$ inch (3 mm) thick.

Fry first the onion and then the mushrooms and parsley in the same butter and when they are nicely browned dust with a little flour and then add the port. Let it bubble for 2–3 minutes and then add the stock, pepper and salt.

Put the kidneys and their onion and mushroom gravy into a small casserole, cover and simmer over a very low heat for 30 minutes. Taste and serve very hot with rice or a creamy potato purée.

Butcher's shop, Barnstaple, North Devon

Braised Oxtail with Haricot Beans

This delicious recipe is derived from *Mrs Manders' Cook Book* published in the USA in 1968. Mrs Manders, cook to British writer Rumer Godden for many years, was given this every Wednesday in the servants' hall of the grand household in which she worked in the 1920s as a housemaid. She recommends port rather than red wine, and I have reduced her four days' preparation to two. If you prefer to soak your beans overnight instead of doing them the quick way, it takes three days. I like oxtail to be overcooked, so that it falls off the bone in succulent pieces. If it isn't quite done, the bones bounce around the plate while you struggle to detach the meat, and it can all be very awkward. The gravy should be gelatinous and very velvety.

Serves 6

2 oxtails, jointed

8 oz (225 g) dried haricot beans

3–4 carrots

2 sticks of celery

2 onions

1 tbsp flour

2 oz (50 g) butter and a little oil

good seasoning of marjoram, thyme and celery salt

2–3 bayleaves

salt and freshly ground pepper

beef stock (optional)

¼ pint (150 ml) red wine or port

THE DAY BEFORE

Soak the oxtails for 2–3 hours. Meanwhile, if you have not soaked them overnight, put the beans in a pan, well covered with water. Bring them to the boil, simmer for 5 minutes and then remove from the heat. Cover the pan and leave it to cool. By the time the beans have cooled down they will be ready to cook. Slice the carrots, celery and peeled onions. Drain and dry the oxtails and dust them with flour.

Heat the butter and oil in a large casserole and fry the pieces of oxtail a few at a time, until they have a nice dark crust. Remove the oxtails, add the sliced vegetables and let them soften for a few minutes. Put back the oxtails, cover with water, add the drained beans, herbs and seasoning and simmer very slowly, with a tilted lid, for 3 hours. Add a little beef stock if the gravy evaporates too rapidly.

Allow to cool and leave overnight in the refrigerator.

THE FOLLOWING DAY

Remove the fat from the top. Add the wine or port and simmer for 1 or 2 hours before serving with puréed celeriac. You can add fresh vegetables for the second half of the cooking if you like.

Fried Calves' Liver and Bacon

allow 4 oz (100 g) calves' liver per person, sliced ¼ inch (0.5 cm) thick

2 rashers smoked back bacon per person

2 tsp olive oil

2 tsp butter

a dusting of flour

salt and freshly ground pepper

Trim the liver, removing the thin membrane from the edges of each slice and any large pipes. Cut the rinds off the bacon and nick the fat with scissors.

Heat the oil and butter in a good, well-seasoned frying pan that doesn't stick. Allow the bacon to cook for about 2 minutes on each side, then transfer it to a heated dish and keep it hot.

Dust the slices of liver lightly with flour and shake off any excess. Put them straight into the hot bacon fat and oil, and brown fairly gently for 2–3 minutes on each side. (Thicker slices will need a little longer.) As you turn the pieces, season the cooked side with salt and pepper.

Serve with the bacon, fried potatoes and perhaps watercress, spinach or a fried tomato.

Lambs' liver can be cooked in exactly the same way; it is best in spring when the new season's lamb comes into the market.

Cattle at Dolton, North Devon

Veal and Ham Pie

This is a rather glorious cornucopia of a pie. When you serve it hot all the filling spills out with a puff of rich, scented steam; delicious cold, it is rather unmanageable for picnics unless you want to take plates, knives and forks with you.

Serves 6

1 lb (450 g) pie veal, cut in large pieces

1 carrot

1 onion, peeled

1 stick of celery

bunch of thyme, parsley and bayleaf

1 pint (550 ml) chicken stock

2 dashes dry white wine

salt and freshly ground pepper

1 lb (450 g) cooked ham in a piece

1½ oz (40 g) butter

1½ oz (40 g) flour

¼ pint (150 ml) double cream

FOR THE LAYER OF MUSHROOMS

8 oz (225 g) tiny white button mushrooms

½ lemon

1 onion

1 oz (25 g) butter

salt and freshly ground pepper

PASTRY

rough puff pastry, using 8 oz (225 g) flour (see page 138)

1 beaten egg, for glazing

flour dredger

First put the veal into a saucepan together with the chopped vegetables, herbs, stock, white wine and just enough water to cover. Bring to the boil, turn down the heat, season and simmer for about 1 hour, until tender. Strain off the stock, remove the herbs and vegetables and reduce the stock to ½ pint (300 ml) by boiling it rapidly. Cut the cooked veal and the ham into fairly small pieces.

TO MAKE THE SAUCE

Melt the butter in a small pan, stir in the flour and let the mixture bubble for a few minutes. Then, away from the heat, add the reduced stock gradually, stirring all the time. Return it to the heat, add the cream, taste for seasoning and cook for a few minutes. Mix it with the veal and ham and allow to cool completely.

Meanwhile, make the mushroom layer.

Clean the mushrooms with half a lemon; if necessary, trim the ends off the stalks. Slice the mushrooms thinly and chop the onion finely. Simmer the onion in butter until soft but not brown, then squeeze a little more lemon over the mushrooms and cook them gently with the onions until all their liquid has evaporated. Season lightly with salt and pepper. Leave to cool.

TO MAKE THE PIE

When both the veal and ham in their sauce and the mushrooms are cold, preheat the oven to 425°F (220°C, Gas 7). Roll out a little less than half of the pastry until you can cut out a round the size of a dinner plate. Place this on a slightly wetted baking sheet and roll out the rest of the pastry slightly larger, but do not cut it yet. Put a layer of half the veal and ham mixture, which should be quite stiff, on to the pastry on the baking sheet, leaving a 1 inch (2.5 cm) margin all round. Cover this with a layer of mushrooms, flattening them with the back of the spoon. Then cover with the remaining veal and ham. Brush the edges of the pastry with water and put the second piece of pastry right over the top. Press it down well all round and trim it to match the piece underneath.

Brush with egg beaten with a little salt and allow to dry before glazing a second time. Decorate with curving radial lines, using a blunt skewer, if you like the look of it. Make a hole in the centre and bake for 25–30 minutes.

Serve hot or cold.

Stewed Veal with Green Peas

This has a delicious old-fashioned flavour, that has been rather forgotten recently. Veal is a very good meat for stewing as it has a gelatinous texture which makes a good velvety gravy.

Serves 4

2 lb (900 g) pie veal

seasoned flour

1 tbsp butter

1 tbsp oil

small glass white wine

4 spring onions, cut into short lengths

bunch of herbs — bay, thyme and parsley

generous pinches of ground mace, allspice, cloves, black pepper

grated rind of $\frac{1}{2}$ lemon

salt and freshly ground pepper

about 1 pint (550 ml) light chicken stock or water

8 oz (225 g) shelled green peas, fresh or frozen

1 tbsp flour worked into 1 oz (25 g) softened butter

2 tsp lemon juice

Cut the veal into large pieces, trimming them well. Roll the pieces in seasoned flour and fry them in the butter and oil in a modest sized casserole a few at a time. Transfer them to a dish when they are lightly browned all over.

Pour the wine into the casserole and scrape up all the sediment. Let it boil for a minute or two, then turn down the heat and throw in the spring onions. Return the veal to the pan and add the herbs, spices and grated lemon rind. Season, add water or stock barely to cover the meat, cover the pan and simmer for 1–1$\frac{1}{2}$ hours or until the veal is meltingly tender.

Meanwhile, cook the peas briefly in boiling salted water. Work the flour into the butter, to make a smooth paste.

When the veal is ready, stir the peas into the gravy and then add half the flour and butter in little pieces, stirring it well over a low heat for several minutes. See if the sauce is as you like it; if it is still too thin, add a little more of the flour and butter paste. Lastly, stir in the lemon juice and taste for seasoning. Serve very hot with boiled new potatoes or mashed potatoes.

Roast Leg of Lamb

'The mountain sheep are sweeter,
But the valley sheep are fatter;
We therefore deemed it meeter
To carry off the latter.'
Thomas Love Peacock (1785–1866) 'The War-song of Dinas Vawr'

Nowadays I think we would carry off the former as nobody likes fat and we think lean meat is healthier, so choose a lean-looking leg. This method allows 15 minutes per lb (450 g) and gives a very succulent, deep rose-pink finish to the lamb when it is carved. For well-done lamb allow 20 minutes per lb (450 g). The resting time allows the meat to relax, making it easier to carve, and gives a more even colour to the slices.

Serves at least 8

1 leg of lamb weighing about 6 lb (2.6 kg), including the knuckle bone

2 oz (50 g) softened butter

3 oz (75 g) fresh white breadcrumbs

3 tbsp chopped parsley

2 tsp dried marjoram

1 tsp dried thyme

$\frac{1}{2}$ tsp salt

FOR THE GRAVY

small wine glass (3 fl oz/75 ml) red wine

$\frac{1}{2}$ pint (300 ml) chicken stock or other stock

A flock at Upcott, North Devon

Preheat the oven to 425°F (220°C, Gas 7).

Spread the lamb all over with butter. Mix together the breadcrumbs, herbs and salt and press them into the butter all over the leg of lamb. (In the past the breadcrumbs and melted butter flavoured with herbs were strewn over the meat as it turned on a spit in front of the fire; this protected the meat from scorching and helped to keep it juicy. This coating forms the same function in the oven.)

Cook on a rack over a roasting tin in the hot oven for 15 minutes, then reduce the heat to 350°F (180°C, Gas 4) and cook for a further 1–1¼ hours. Allow the lamb to rest in a warm place for ½ hour before carving.

TO MAKE THE GRAVY

While the lamb is resting, take the roasting tin which has caught all the juices and falling crumbs. Spoon off most of the fat and add the red wine. Bring the liquid to the boil, let it reduce by half and then add the chicken stock or other good, well-flavoured stock. Reduce again, stirring the bottom of the tin to release all the syrupy, caramelised juices that have collected there. When reduced to about half, strain the gravy into a heated gravy-boat and serve very, very hot with the lamb sliced fairly thickly if very pink, and thinly if well done. Serve with scalloped potatoes and roast winter vegetables in winter, and new potatoes and peas, or, even better, runner beans, in summer.

Roast Saddle of Lamb

This is a dish for an expert carver. If you ask the butcher how to tackle it, he will be pleased to explain, and if you then provide yourself with a very sharp knife, you will be halfway there.

Serves 10

1 saddle of lamb weighing about 10 lb (4.5 kg)

2–3 oz (50–75 g) softened butter

salt and freshly ground pepper

1 oz (25 g) flour

¼ pint (150 ml) port

½ pint (300 ml) stock made from lamb bones

pinch of sugar

1 tsp red wine vinegar (optional)

2 lemons

cayenne pepper

Preheat the oven to 375°F (190°C, Gas 5).

Remove the kidneys from the back of the saddle and protect the tail with a piece of foil. Put the saddle in a roasting tin, coat with butter and season. Roast for 12 minutes per lb (450 g), basting it once or twice. Put the kidneys into the tin about 30 minutes before the end of the cooking time, tucking them under the lamb so that they do not dry out.

Remove the lamb from the oven and take off the foil. Put the kidneys back on either side of the tail, secured with cocktail sticks. Cover the whole saddle with foil and let it rest.

Remove most of the fat from the roasting tin. Add the flour and brown it, stirring to collect all the caramelised juices. Add the port and let it sizzle for a minute or two before you stir in the stock. Add a pinch of salt, a pinch of sugar and, if you wish, 1 tsp red wine vinegar, and cook for a few minutes.

TO SERVE

Place the lamb on a serving dish with quartered lemons around it, and sprinkle it lightly with cayenne pepper. Brush it with melted butter to make it shine. Serve with the gravy, mint sauce, redcurrant jelly, new potatoes and tiny peas.

Lamb Chops or Cutlets

Looking at recipes for lamb chops and lamb cutlets makes me realise that nothing is better than a lamb cutlet plainly grilled. For example St James's Club lamb cutlets have a slit made in the thick part into which is piped some foie gras. They are then dipped in egg and crumbs and fried, and served with rich brown sauce. Reform Club lamb cutlets are coated with chopped ham, parsley and crumbs, then egg and crumbed, then fried and served with julienne of ham, truffle, gherkin, hard-boiled egg and so forth and a little demi-glace sauce with redcurrant jelly in it. Cutlets à la Pall Mall are stewed in onion purée and seasoned with cayenne and lemon or garlic vinegar. All the London clubs had their own particular recipe, each one as complicated as these and only to be enjoyed when someone else is doing the cooking. At home, cutlets grilled or fried are best.

So I will repeat the words of Mrs Philip Martineau from her book *Caviare to Candy* written in 1927:

TO FRY CHOPS OR CUTLETS
One should aim at getting a juicy chop rather pink (and certainly not grey) in the middle, and dark brown without, and this can only be done by searing the meat; that is to say, by subjecting it quickly to a great heat for a minute or two each side.
When a grill is in use, do not try any other method, otherwise use a heavy iron frying pan. Grease it lightly and make it very, very hot over the fire. Place your chops or cutlets (or steak) on the frying pan which is almost dry, and let them sear for a few minutes. When one side is seared brown, turn it with a wooden spoon and do the other side brown. Keep turning every few minutes from one side to the other, and never stick a fork into the meat for fear the juice should run out. They will not take very long to cook, and should be served quickly and hot, with a sprinkle of salt and pepper on them, and on a very hot plate. No gravy is needed, though a little pat of butter on each is appreciated.'

Incidentally, Edward VII liked mayonnaise with his lamb chops — which is actually quite well worth a try.

Lamb Curry

Serves 4–6

2 lb (900 g) shoulder of lamb, cubed, fat removed (weighed after trimming — this is the quantity you will get from 1 shoulder)

---

3 onions

---

3 cloves garlic

2–3 tbsp oil or softened butter

---

2 tbsp hot Madras curry powder

---

2 tsp curry paste

---

2 tsp ground coriander

---

1 tsp ground cumin

$\frac{1}{2}$ tsp or less ground chilli ($\frac{1}{2}$ tsp makes it very hot)

---

1 inch (2.5 cm) cube fresh ginger, chopped finely

---

1 pint (550 ml) lamb stock (made preferably from the bones and trimmings of the shoulder), well skimmed

---

$1\frac{1}{2}$ tsp salt

---

2 tbsp coconut milk (optional, see right)

Trim the meat well and peel and chop the onions and garlic. Heat the oil or butter and fry the onions and garlic until pale golden. Add the curry powder and paste and spices and fry for a minute or two, then add the ginger and the meat. Fry over a moderate heat so the meat is browned and sealed on all sides. Add the lamb stock and salt, and a little coconut milk, if using.

Bring to a simmer and cook gently on top of the stove or in the oven at 325°F (170°C, Gas 3) for $1\frac{1}{2}$ hours or until tender. Stir frequently and allow the liquid to cook down until it is rich and thick — just enough to bathe the meat; this curry is a dryish one rather than a wet one.

TO SERVE

Serve with hot lemon pickle or hot lime pickle and mango chutney, and with rice. Other good side dishes to serve with this curry are quartered lemons, some shredded lettuce with quartered tomatoes and fried poppadums. Prawn bulachao — a hot chutney made with dried prawns — is also delicious.

TO MAKE COCONUT MILK

Pour $2\frac{1}{2}$ fl oz (60 ml) boiling water over $1\frac{1}{2}$ tbsp desiccated coconut. Allow to steep for 5 minutes, then sieve, pressing the coconut to extract all the juice. Use in chicken, prawn and lamb curry.

Irish Stew

'There was an old man of Peru
Who watched his wife making a stew;
But once by mistake, in a stove she did bake
That unfortunate man of Peru.'
from THE COMPLETE NONSENSE OF EDWARD LEAR

This is real peasant food, the easiest thing to make and it does taste absolutely wonderful. Do not worry about the look of it when you first take it out of the oven, the parsley tones it up and adds a final freshness to the mellow flavour. Use only very good lamb, and have the bones well trimmed.

Serves 4

1½–2 lb (675–900 g) best end and middle neck of
    English lamb, cut into chops and well trimmed

1 lb (450 g) potatoes

8 oz (225 g) onions

salt and freshly ground pepper

thyme

¾ pint (425 ml) good home-made stock

freshly chopped parsley

Preheat the oven to 325°F (170°C, Gas 3).
    Cut all the larger pieces of fat away from the chops. Peel the potatoes, cutting them into fairly large pieces, and peel and chop the onions rather coarsely.
    Put a layer of chops in a 4 pint (2.2 litre) casserole, season them well with salt, pepper and thyme. Then put in a layer of onions and a layer of potatoes. Repeat these three layers, add stock, cover the pot with a piece of buttered foil and the lid, and cook for at least 2 hours or until the meat is really tender.
    Serve the stew sprinkled with liberal quantities of fresh chopped parsley.

Shepherd's Pie

Shepherd's pie is always made with leftover roast lamb and can be delicious, juicy and full of flavour, or dry and boring according to how much trouble you take. Cottage pie is the same sort of thing but made with beef — either fresh minced beef or cold roast beef. You can use the same recipe with either.

Serves 6

1½ lb (675 g) roast lamb (preferably underdone)

2 onions

1 tbsp vegetable oil

1 oz (25 g) butter

1 oz (25 g) flour

4 tbsp red wine

8 fl oz (225 ml) gravy or stock

½ tsp dried thyme

½ tsp well pounded dried rosemary

Tabasco sauce

1 tsp tomato purée

salt and freshly ground black pepper

FOR THE MASHED POTATO

1½ lb (675 g) potatoes

2 oz (50 g) butter

¼ pint (150 ml) hot milk

salt and freshly ground black pepper

MAKE THE MASHED POTATOES

Cook the potatoes in well-salted water until very tender, drain well and mash adding plenty of butter and hot milk. Give them a good beating to make them really smooth and creamy and season well.

Mincing machine, from
Household Management, c. 1880

FOR THE FILLING

Mince or chop the lamb not too finely (coarser pieces do not dry out so quickly). Peel and chop the onions. Heat the oil and butter in a large frying pan and fry the onions until golden brown. Add the lamb and let it brown in places, then sprinkle on the flour and brown that too as much as is possible — most of it disappears into the meat in some mysterious way. Now add the liquids, first the red wine which should bubble and sizzle, then the stock. Stir it in well, deglazing the pan, and add the herbs and seasonings, including the Tabasco and tomato purée. Simmer for about 10 minutes, add more stock if necessary then transfer to a 9 inch (23 cm) pie dish.

Cover lightly with mashed potato — do not smooth it down. Dot the top all over with little bits of butter and cook at 350°F (180°C, Gas 4) for 30 minutes or until nicely browned and crusty on top.

Boiled Bacon

'Some other meat you may have, but bacon is the great thing. It is always ready; as good cold as hot; goes to the field or coppice conveniently; in harvest, and other busy times, demands the pot to be boiled only on a Sunday; has twice as much strength in it as any other thing of the same weight; and in short has in it every quality that tends to make a labourer's family able to work and be well off.'
William Cobbett COTTAGE ECONOMY 1830

Bacon for boiling comes from the middle and fore-end of the pig, while gammon and ham come from the hind leg. Boiling bacon, gammon, and the back and streaky bacon that we fry in our old black frying pan for breakfast, can all have the same cure, of which there are many variations, and can all be green (unsmoked) or smoked. They are usually quite salty and will need to be soaked overnight before boiling, preferably with several changes of water.

Because they are fatter than gammon, fore-end cuts of boiling bacon are cheaper. They are also less likely to get dry in cooking and are delicious cold. I think when we were children, during the Second World War, we would have given all our sugar ration for a bit of boiled bacon; we ate it fat and all. Indeed in Cobbett's day and even up to the 1930s every cottager kept a huge pig and cold boiled fat bacon and bread was his favourite daily food.

Cook boiled bacon exactly like gammon. For 6 people soak a piece weighing about 2½–3 lb (1.1–1.3 kg) overnight and simmer it with leeks, celery and root vegetables or onions, and a bunch of herbs, for 30 minutes per lb (450 g) for a small joint (less for a larger one, see table page 72). Use the boiling liquid to make pea or split pea or lentil soup.

TO SERVE

Serve the boiled bacon hot with its skin removed, with parsley sauce, and then cold with mustard, into which you can stir a little honey if you like.

Cooking a Gammon or Ham

'... My salads, roots and pot-herbs, my own garden yields in plenty and perfection; the produce of the natural soil, prepared by moderate cultivation. The same soil affords all the different fruits which England can call her own so that my dessert is every day fresh-gathered from the tree; my dairy flows with nectareous tides of milk and cream, from which derive abundance of excellent butter, curds and cheese; and the refuse fattens my pigs, that are destined for hams and bacon.'
Tobias Smollett THE EXPEDITION OF HUMPHREY CLINKER 1771

Many people are in a state of confusion about what is gammon and what is ham. Technically gammon is a joint cut from the hind quarter of a side of bacon, while for ham the hind quarter is cut and cured separately from the rest of the pig. Speciality hams such as York, Bradenham, or Suffolk are still cut and cured separately by traditional methods. You will find, however, that it is perfectly correct nowadays to call the cured hind leg of the bacon pig gammon when it is served hot, but ham when cold.

A small piece of gammon or uncooked ham takes more time to cook per pound than a large one. Anything under 5 lb (2.2 kg) takes 30 minutes per lb (450 g) and 30 minutes over. We usually buy a piece weighing about 5 lb (2.2 kg) and I allow 30 minutes per lb (450 g) without extra time. Anything over this gets a relatively shorter time. These times come from a chart compiled by the Ministry of Agriculture and Fisheries, and reproduced in Jane Grigson's *Charcuterie and French Pork Cookery*.

5–10 lb (2.2–4.4 kg)	2½ hours
10 lb (4.4 kg)	3 hours
12 lb (5.2 kg)	3½ hours
14 lb (6.3 kg)	3¾ hours
16 lb (7.2 kg)	4 hours
18 lb (8.1 kg)	4¼ hours
20 lb (9 kg)	4½ hours
22 lb (9.9 kg)	4¾ hours
24 lb (10.8 kg)	5 hours

Weigh the joint before soaking to calculate the time you will have to allow. There is nothing more disappointing than very salty ham, so always soak the ham or gammon thoroughly unless your butcher specifically tells you it will not need it; always check if possible. Soak a small piece, under 4 lb (1.8 kg) overnight: a larger, 5–10 lb (2.2–4.4 kg) piece for 24 hours, changing the water frequently. A whole ham will need 3 days' soaking and a Bradenham ham takes up to a week to soak properly. Change the water regularly and keep it in a cool place or it may go off.

When it is ready to cook, put the joint into a large pan and cover with cold water. Bring to the boil, then turn down the heat to a simmer, skim and add a carrot, 2 leeks, a couple of onions and sticks of celery and a bunch of herbs. Count the cooking time from this point. Like all so called 'boiled' meat, ham should never be boiled, but gently simmered with a nice rhythmic, lazy 'blop' coming up at intervals as you watch. Taste the liquid occasionally and if it starts to taste unpalatably salty in spite of all your soaking, change it, adding fresh boiling water to replace it.

Test the meat with a skewer when it is time for it to be done; it should feel quite firm but not rubbery. Remove the pan from the heat.

TO SERVE HOT

If you want to glaze it, remove the ham from its cooking liquid about 30 minutes before the end of the cooking time. Lift it out on to a dish and remove the skin, leaving the fat intact. Score the fat in a diamond pattern, stick a clove into each intersection and coat with a glaze such as the one opposite. Pour a little oil and perhaps a few tablespoons of apple juice or of the cooking liquid into a roasting tin, put the ham, fat side up, on top, and roast at 375°F (190°C, Gas 5) for 20–30 minutes or until glazed a rich, shiny, mahogany colour. Serve this with Cumberland sauce or parsley sauce.

Alternatively, you can complete the cooking in the water, then simply remove the skin and serve the joint as it is.

TO SERVE COLD

Either glaze the ham as above, and let it get cold, or let it cool in the cooking liquid, then remove it. Take off the skin, dry the fat and press fine dried breadcrumbs into it all over — use home-made

Pigs enjoying the sun, Iddesleigh, North Devon

breadcrumbs, the bought ones are a horrible bright orange and make everything look the same.

For a whole ham, either buy a frill to put over the knuckle, which makes it easy to hold whilst you are carving, or make one out of white paper. If you are keeping a cooked ham for a period of time and continuing to cut from it, keep the cut surface covered to prevent it drying out.

Serve the ham with Cumberland sauce or with home-made chutney, baked potatoes and salad — chicory and orange is good.

Glaze for Gammon or Ham

For a 3–4 lb (1.3–1.8 kg) gammon or ham.

3 tsp mustard — I use Dijon

grated rind of a lemon or orange

squeeze of lemon or orange juice, or a little cider vinegar

1 oz (25 g) soft dark brown sugar

Mix all the ingredients together in a bowl and spread over the outside of the skinned and scored ham (see opposite). Roast at 375°F (190°C, Gas 5) for 20–30 minutes, checking to see that the top does not burn. Cover it with a piece of foil if it gets too dark.

Roast Loin of Pork with Crackling

The best part of the loin is the piece with the kidney underneath.

Serves 6

3½–4 lb (1.5–1.8 kg) loin of pork, with the bone chined and skin scored by the butcher

½ oz (15 g) butter

2 tbsp oil

FOR THE GRAVY

½ tbsp flour

1 tbsp sherry

½–1 small wine glass (1½–3 fl oz/35–75 ml) red wine

1 bayleaf

¼ pint (150 ml) stock

salt and freshly ground pepper

It is best not to overcook pork; unfortunately, because it is common knowledge that it should not be eaten underdone, it is nearly always overdone. You want to cook it only until it has a white, pearly sheen (it is pink when underdone and pale beige when overdone). It should still be succulent and juicy, but the crackling should be very crisp.

Start by preheating the oven to 425°F (220°C, Gas 7). Rub the crackling with a little piece of butter — it gives a better result than oil. Don't sprinkle it with salt, this will toughen the crackling. Put the remaining butter and oil in a roasting tin with the pork on top.

Roast the pork at the high temperature for 10–15 minutes then turn down the heat to 375°F (190°C, Gas 5). From this point allow 20 minutes to 1 lb (450 g) and 20 minutes over for a small joint. Don't baste the crackling, just let it cook and it will be crisp and delicious by the end.

When the joint is ready, transfer it to a serving dish, keep it hot and let it rest for about 15 minutes while you make the gravy. Spoon some of the fat off the roasting tin if necessary, then sprinkle in the flour and let it brown, stirring up all the sediment. Add the sherry, red wine and bayleaf, keep cooking it over a medium heat until reduced somewhat, then add the stock half at a time, stirring and tasting. Add seasoning and serve with the pork. It should be delicious, especially if you use good rich stock.

TO SERVE

Onion and sage sauce is the traditional accompaniment but I prefer to serve apple and sage sauce — just sprinkle a little chopped sage in with the baked apple sauce on page 143.

Home-made Pork Pie

'There is nothing to equal a good English farmhouse pork pie, if the crust is not, as it all too often is, thick heavy and stodgy. Flaky crust should merge imperceptibly into doughy, the doughy into jelly that is not extraneous to the meat employed and the jelly into the meat, like mingling geological strata.'
P. Morton Shand A BOOK OF FOOD 1927

The pork pie is a real institution, the favourite lunch, along with a ploughman's lunch, of most English pub-goers. Many pies are bought to eat at home too, especially at weekends; and as for picnics, who would want to go without one? To make a pork pie, on the other hand, is almost unheard of, although it can be extremely enjoyable. The instructions here are for a hand-raised pie, but some people find it easier to use a mould.

Serves 6–8

1 lb (450 g) belly of pork

4 oz (100 g) streaky bacon

1 lb (450 g) pork bones and trimmings

2 bayleaves

2 leaves of red sage

10 black peppercorns

1 lb (450 g) boneless pork shoulder or loin

2 scant tsp salt

pepper and nutmeg

1 egg, for glazing

HOT WATER CRUST PASTRY

1 lb (450 g) plain flour
5 oz (150 g) lard, diced
2 pinches salt

Remove the rinds from the belly of pork and streaky bacon. Put them with the bones and any other trimmings into a pan with the bayleaves, sage leaves and peppercorns; cover with water and make stock by simmering gently until clear, reduced by half and deliciously flavoured. Strain this stock and return it to the pan to reduce again, ending up with about $\frac{1}{2}$ pint (300 ml). Allow to cool, when it will set to a jelly, and remove the fat from the top.

Chop the bacon and two kinds of pork by hand or in a food processor. Chop one third finely, leaving two thirds rather coarsely chopped. Mix with the salt, a lot of coarse black pepper (at least 20 turns of the peppermill) and a good deal of grated nutmeg.

TO MAKE THE PASTRY

Bring the lard and $\frac{1}{4}$ pint (150 ml) water to the boil in a saucepan. If you are using a hinged pie mould you can increase the quantity of fat up to half the weight of flour, but use the amounts suggested in the ingredients above for a hand-raised pie, as it makes the pastry easier to handle.

Put the flour and salt into a bowl and as soon as the lard and water mixture boils, pour it into the middle and mix it together with a spoon. As soon as it is cool enough to handle, knead it well and cover it with a cloth. Leave it in a warm place to rest for 20 minutes. Now cut off one quarter of the dough and leave it in a warm place, wrapped up.

SHAPING THE PIE

Put the rest of the dough on a greased baking sheet, spread it out a little and put a jar about $4\frac{1}{2}$ inches across by 6 inches high (11 x 15 cm) in the middle. With your hands, work the dough up the sides of the jar until it is within an inch (2.5 cm) of the top. Tie double greaseproof paper round the pie and put it in the refrigerator to chill for a while.

Preheat the oven to 350°F (180°C, Gas 4). Now put a teatowel in the jar and pour on boiling water, enough to soak the cloth. The next step is easier with two people — one holds the pie whilst the

other twists the jar and lifts it out, the heat will have released it. Pack in the pork mixture; make sure it is even or the pie may tip over. Roll out the remaining pastry, and cut a round lid about $\frac{1}{4}$ inch (6 mm) wider in diameter than the base of the jar. Make a hole in the centre. Paint the edges with beaten egg glaze, place the lid on top of the pie and pinch the edges together to make a scalloped rim.

BAKING AND FINISHING

Bake the pie for 1 hour, remove the greaseproof paper and brush all over with egg glaze. Cook for a further 15–20 minutes. Allow to cool, then chill for 1 hour.

Have your jellied stock at warm room temperature, when it is syrupy but not quite set. Pour it through a funnel into the cold pie through the hole in the pastry. Allow to set in a cool larder or the bottom of the refrigerator overnight, but take the pie out at least an hour before you want to eat it. It should be a triumph of pie-making.

TO SERVE

Serve with a superlative green salad, some fresh tomatoes, and beer.

ALTERNATIVE

You can put one hard-boiled egg right in the middle of this pie; it looks very pretty when cut.

Pie mould, from *Good Plain Cookery* by Mary Hooper, 1882

To Roast a Chicken — A Family Recipe

This is a traditional plain golden roast bird with a light stuffing, very much nicer and more delicate than a dense solid one. You can add grated lemon rind and chopped parsley or marjoram to the stuffing if you like, and also the chopped chicken liver, fried with a little chopped onion. Use the neck, gizzard and heart to make the stock.

Serves 4

1 chicken weighing 3 lb (1.3 kg), free-range if possible

2–3 tbsp fresh breadcrumbs

salt and freshly ground black pepper

2½ oz (60 g) butter

a dusting of flour

FOR THE GRAVY

3–4 tbsp chicken stock

2–3 tbsp double cream

2 tsp sherry

Preheat the oven to 375°F (190°C, Gas 5). Remove any rubber bands or giblets in plastic bags from your chicken, they will not improve the flavour. Fill the cavity with breadcrumbs, brown or white, seasoned with salt and plenty of pepper. Add 1 oz (25 g) butter and truss the legs with string.

Put the chicken in a roasting tin, cover the breast with flakes of butter and with a piece of buttered greaseproof paper. Put the remaining butter in the tin. Roast, lifting the paper to baste the bird once or twice.

After 1 hour remove the paper, dust the bird with flour and baste with juices from the roasting tin. Return to the oven, uncovered, for 15 minutes to crisp and brown.

Meanwhile, make a little concentrated stock with the chicken giblets. (Make sure you trim off any greenish patches on the liver, as they taste bitter.)

TO MAKE THE GRAVY

Test the bird by pricking the thick part of the leg with a needle or skewer. If the juices run colourless and clear it is cooked. Remove the chicken from the roasting tin and keep hot while you add the stock to the juices in the tin. Boil it fast for 2–3 minutes, scraping up the juices. Then add the cream and sherry and boil until it reaches a good consistency. Remember when you are carving to give each person a spoonful of the breadcrumbs from inside the bird — they are delicious.

Hole Farm, North Devon

Chicken Salad

There are many recipes for chicken salad with curry, some vastly complicated like the one described in *Lady Sysonby's Cook Book* in 1935 (a nice little book with illustrations by Oliver Messel). In this apples, onions, potatoes, tomatoes, raw rice and celery are stewed in 8 oz (225 g) butter and then boiled for an hour with curry powder. This is then puréed and mixed with whipped cream, the juice of a lemon and mayonnaise and used to cover a cold boiled chicken cut in well-shaped pieces. Another complex one includes mayonnaise, chicken stock and apricot jam, when it becomes Coronation Chicken or Chicken Elizabeth.

But I feel that on a hot day one wants to spend as much time as possible in a wicker chair outdoors under the trees and not much in the kitchen, so I have given a really simple recipe that takes only a few minutes to make and is fresh, delicate and very good to eat.

Serves 6

1 cold, freshly roasted chicken

¼ pint (150 ml) home-made mayonnaise, made with a light vegetable oil such as arachide, and lemon juice

1 tsp hot curry powder

1 tsp lemon juice

2–3 tbsp lightly whipped cream

salt and pepper

4 long sprigs of fresh tarragon, chopped

You can either take the chicken off the bones or cut it into joints. Make sure it is completely cool or it will melt the mayonnaise and be rather limp. Put it into a bowl.

Mix the lemon juice, curry powder and cream into the mayonnaise and taste for seasoning. Stir in the chopped tarragon and pour it over the chicken. Turn the pieces over until they are coated. Serve with lettuce hearts and cold rice and with mango chutney if you like.

Josefa's Chicken Curry

Serves 4

1 chicken

2 onions

1½ inch (4 cm) piece of fresh root ginger

2–3 small green chillies

3 large cloves garlic

3 tbsp vegetable oil

3 tbsp curry powder — preferably Bolsts' hot

¾ pint (425 ml) milk, or coconut milk, page 69

salt and freshly ground pepper

1–2 tsp chutney (orange chutney, page 148, is good)

FOR THE SIDE DISHES

2 hard-boiled eggs, chopped

2 tomatoes, skinned and chopped

2–3 oz (50–75 g) roasted peanuts or cashew nuts

½ onion, peeled and chopped

2 bananas, sliced

Cut the chicken into 8 neat pieces. Chop the peeled onions, the ginger, seeded chillies and garlic finely. (Take care to wash your hands after handling chillies.)

Heat the oil in a casserole and fry the chicken until pale golden on all sides. Remove the pieces. Lower the heat and fry the onions, garlic, chillies, ginger and curry powder, until the onions are soft. Return the chicken to the casserole and pour on the milk. Add salt, pepper and chutney and simmer fairly rapidly for 40 minutes, until the chicken is cooked through.

TO SERVE

Put the ingredients for the side dishes separately into little bowls. Serve the curry with plenty of rice and hand the side dishes round.

A weatherboarded granary supported on staddle stones at Grange Farm, Basing, Hampshire

Charter Pie

'The first course was, part of a large Cod, a Chine of Mutton, some Soup, a Chicken Pye, Puddings and Roots, etc. Second course, Pidgeons and Asparagus. A Fillet of Veal with Mushrooms and high Sauce with it, rosted Sweetbreads, hot Lobster, Apricot Tart and in the Middle a Pyramid of Syllabubs and Jellies. We had Dessert of Fruit after Dinner and Madeira, White Port and red to drink as Wine. We were all very cheerful and merry.'
The Reverend James Woodforde THE DIARY OF A COUNTRY PARSON 1758–81, entry for 20 April 1774

I find, happily, we can all be cheerful and merry with nothing but this chicken pie for the main course. Cream, parsley and mignonette pepper make a delicious sauce for it. A cold version called Carbery pie is made by leaving out the flour and butter from the sauce; the stock with its cream will set to a nice creamy jelly when cold.

Serves 6

1 roasting chicken, weighing about $3\frac{1}{2}$ lb (1.5 kg)

2 sticks of celery

1 onion

2 leeks

bouquet of herbs — parsley, thyme and bayleaf

3 tbsp white wine

salt

1 oz (25 g) butter

1 oz (25 g) flour

1 tsp coarsely crushed *white* peppercorns (see page 144)

$\frac{1}{4}$ pint (150 ml) double cream

3 tbsp chopped parsley

rough puff pastry made with 6 oz (175 g) flour (see page 138)

egg, for glazing

Put the chicken into a saucepan which fits it fairly closely. Cover it with water and bring it to the boil. Reduce the heat to a simmer, skimming well. Then add the celery, onion, leeks and herbs, wine and seasoning and simmer steadily for 1 hour.

Lift out the chicken, strain the stock and return it to the pan to reduce by boiling to $\frac{1}{2}$ pint (300 ml).

Remove the chicken from the bones and put the pieces into a 10 inch (25 cm) pie dish with a pie funnel in the middle.

Make a sauce with the butter, flour, stock from the chicken and the mignonette (coarsely crushed) white pepper. This is very important for the eventual flavour of the pie.

Add the cream and at least 3 tbsp chopped parsley. Pour it over the chicken and fold it in so that all the chicken is coated with it. Allow to cool.

Preheat the oven to 425°F (220°C, Gas 7). Cover the pie with a crust (see the recipe for steak and kidney pie, page 57), glaze and bake in the preheated oven for 10 minutes. Then reduce the heat to 350°F (180°C, Gas 4) and bake for a further 20 minutes or more; at this moderate heat it will not spoil if it has to wait until you are ready for it.

Chicken Croquettes and Rissoles

Chicken croquettes are best made with freshly roasted chicken. At their finest and most delicate they are superb, creamy and well-flavoured inside, crisp and light on the outside. They are, however, a fiddle to make, so there is an alternative recipe for making the same mixture into rissoles; Francis Bacon remembers his mother, a superlative cook, serving what she called 'reesoles' that were the most wonderful delicacies. As with so many English dishes, rissoles fell into bad repute when they were used to disguise boring leftovers, but properly made with cold roast chicken or pink roast beef, they can be extremely good. Serve them with a fresh tomato sauce.

Serves 4

meat of $\frac{1}{2}$ chicken or 1 small chicken, roasted (or leftover roast chicken)

$\frac{1}{2}$ pint (300 ml) stiff, well-flavoured béchamel sauce made with:
    $1\frac{1}{2}$ oz (40 g) butter
    $1\frac{1}{2}$ oz (40 g) flour
    $\frac{1}{4}$ pint (150 ml) good chicken stock
    $\frac{1}{4}$ pint (150 ml) creamy milk
    salt and freshly ground pepper

a large handful of parsley

4 oz (100 g) very crisp white button mushrooms

1 oz (25 g) butter

flour

1 egg, beaten

freshly made breadcrumbs

oil for frying

1 lemon

Cut the chicken into tiny pieces and mix them and a tablespoon of chopped parsley into the stiff béchamel sauce. Chop the mushrooms fairly coarsely and soften in a little butter, without browning them; stir into the chicken mixture, season well and allow to get very cold in the refrigerator.

CROQUETTES
Shape the mixture into cork shapes with well-floured hands, then dip first into beaten egg and then into crumbs. Deep fry at 350°F (180°C) until golden, crisp and cooked, turning them over once. Serve with quartered lemons and deep fried parsley, well drained, and watercress sauce (page 144); or with parsley sauce (page 143).

RISSOLES
Form the chilled mixture into small hamburger shapes with floured hands. Shallow fry in oil and butter and serve with tomato sauce or ketchup.

Turkeys at Millhams, North Devon

Turkey with Prunes

'Dr Trusler in 1788 wrote: "We are always in pain for a man who, instead of cutting up a fowl genteely, is hacking for half an hour across a bone, greasing himself and bespattering the company with the sauce." Not every unskilled carver had the aplomb of the man who knocked the bird he was carving into his neighbour's lap, but finished the story he was telling before turning to her and saying "Madame, I'll thank you for that turkey".'
Helen Morris PORTRAIT OF A CHEF — THE LIFE OF ALEXIS SOYER, SOMETIME CHEF TO THE REFORM CLUB 1938

Make the stock for the gravy the day before so that you can take off all the fat. When it has been in the refrigerator the fat sets in a layer on top that you can just lift off with a spoon. Put the prunes to soak the day before, too.

Serves 10–12

15 lb (6.8 kg) turkey, all feather stubs removed

2 dozen prunes

2–3 tbsp port or sherry

4 oz (100 g) smoked streaky bacon in a piece

2 oz (50 g) good quality walnut halves, or better still freshly shelled walnuts

salt and freshly ground pepper

4 oz (100 g) butter

30 small onions (2 lb/900 g), preferably silver onions

4 tsp icing sugar

FOR THE STOCK

turkey giblets

4 oz (100 g) stewing beef

2 chicken wings or 2 sets of chicken giblets

1 large onion stuck with a clove

1 bayleaf

12 black peppercorns

a little salt

FOR THE GRAVY

¼ pint (150 ml) red wine or sherry

1 tsp potato flour

knob of butter

salt and freshly ground pepper

THE DAY BEFORE

Put all the stock ingredients in a large pan with plenty of cold water. Bring to the boil, skim off the scum then simmer it very, very slowly for about 2 hours, uncovered to keep it clear. Strain, leaving all sediment behind, and keep ready in the refrigerator. If it seems weak, strengthen the flavour by boiling to reduce the quantity.

Soak the prunes overnight in a little water and 2–3 tbsp port or sherry.

ON THE DAY

Preheat the oven to 350°F (180°C, Gas 4). Drain the prunes. Cut the bacon into sticks and blanch in boiling water for 2–3 minutes; drain and brown lightly in a small frying pan.

Fill the turkey with prunes, walnuts and bacon, season lightly and sew or skewer the opening and, if necessary, truss the legs together with string. Put in the roasting tin with 4 tbsp water and cover the breast and legs with 2 oz (50 g) butter cut in flakes.

Roast for 3¼–3½ hours, turning and basting it every half an hour. When it is a beautiful, even brown, cover with buttered geaseproof paper (not foil) and finish roasting.

GLAZED ONIONS

Meanwhile, peel the onions and put in a wide pan in one layer. Add 2 oz (50 g) butter, the sugar, ¼ pint (150 ml) water and a pinch of salt. Cook, turning frequently, until the water has evaporated and the onions are coated with a brown syrupy glaze. Keep aside in this pan ready to reheat.

THE GRAVY

When the turkey is cooked, remove it from the roasting tin to its dish, first draining any liquid from the inside into the tin.

Remove most of the fat from the tin and add the wine or sherry and several generous ladles of stock. Blend the potato flour with 1–2 tbsp cold water. Stir it into the gravy and bring to the boil, stirring all the time and scraping the tin well. Cook for 5 minutes, adding more stock as necessary. The gravy should be glossy, dark brown and rich. Season well and you can stir in a knob of butter at this point for a very velvety sauce.

TO SERVE
Remove the string or skewers from the turkey and carefully take out the prunes, bacon and walnuts with a spoon. Pile them, mixed with the hot glazed onions, round the front of the turkey on its serving dish.

Serve with crusty roast potatoes, Brussels sprouts with fried breadcrumbs (3 oz/75 g fresh breadcrumbs fried in 2 oz/50 g butter), the giblet gravy and cranberry jelly.

CHESTNUT STUFFING
You can stuff the front of the turkey with a conventional chestnut and sausagemeat stuffing. To make this buy 1 lb (450 g) of the best sausages you can find, skin them and put the sausagemeat into a bowl. Add an egg, 10 chestnuts, boiled, shelled and skinned (see page 86), 2 chopped shallots fried in butter, and seasonings of pepper, salt, nutmeg and chopped parsley. Fry a little of this to check the seasoning, and then use it to stuff the front end of the turkey under the neck skin. Use a skewer to fasten the natural pocket made by the flap, so that it does not come undone.

Roast Grouse with Lettuce Hearts

Grouse come into season in August, a happy moment for lovers of game. For this recipe you must have the tight-hearted crisp little lettuces that grow in the late summer or early autumn (called Butter-crunch), or small Cos lettuces.

Serves 4

4 young grouse
a sprinkling of flour
4 oz (100 g) butter
4 rashers bacon, rinds removed
$\frac{1}{4}$ pint (150 ml) red wine
$\frac{1}{4}$ pint (150 ml) game or chicken stock
3–4 lettuces, all outside leaves removed
salt and freshly ground pepper

Preheat the oven to 425°F (220°C, Gas 7).

Dust the grouse with flour, put a little nut of butter and a sprinkling of salt and pepper inside each one, and fry them in the remaining butter in a small roasting pan until they are sealed and golden brown all over. Then cover the breasts with rashers of bacon hammered thin with a rolling pin and cut in half.

Place the roasting tin with the grouse in the hot oven. After 8–10 minutes baste them, turn down the heat to 350°F (180°C, Gas 4) and cook for a further 15 minutes. Keep them hot on a serving dish, surrounded with the bacon.

Skim the fat off the juices in the roasting tin, add the wine and simmer uncovered to reduce to 2–3 tbsp. Then add the stock and reduce again until the flavour is rich enough for your taste. Taste for seasoning and put into a hot gravy boat.

TO SERVE
Quarter the lettuce hearts and serve each person with a grouse and three or four quarters of lettuce heart with the roasting juices poured over. The combination of the gravy and hearts of lettuce is quite delicious.

Colonel Birdwood and Colonel Graham waiting for a woodcock, Hearton Satchville, Huish

Roast Partridge

'The partridge is a bird that most of us secretly prefer to pheasant. The latter is admittedly far more economically satisfactory, but there is something genial and lovable about the partridge which is lacking in the pheasant . . . on occasion there is no better menu for a victim of despondency.'
Major Hugh B.C. Pollard GAME BIRDS 1929

Partridge are delicate little birds with a much less gamey flavour than grouse. Of the two kinds, grey-legged and red-legged, the grey-legged are thought to be superior. Since they are somewhat pale fleshed they are not so appetising if they are seriously under-done.

Serve 1 partridge per person

Fill each bird with a knob of butter rolled in salt and pepper, dust them with flour, and brown them quickly in butter and olive oil. Then tie bacon over the breasts and roast them in a hottish oven 400–425°F (200–220°C, Gas 6–7), for 20 minutes for a pinkish bird, 25 for a well-done one. Allow a little less if they are very small, more if very large — the medium ones are about the size of a pigeon. Remove the bacon before serving.

TO SERVE
Serve with gravy made with pan juices and perhaps watercress, game chips (page 100) and a couple of braised endives. A fried-bread croûte, large enough for the bird to sit on and spread with a paste made with the bird's livers, fried in butter and flavoured with a few drops of brandy, can be put underneath each partridge. The bread will absorb its delicious juices and taste quite wonderful.

Game for sale in Butchers Row, Barnstaple, North Devon

Ducks at Millhams, North Devon

Roast Duck

Ducks are notoriously difficult to carve. Either do it beforehand in the kitchen, or get someone who knows their anatomy to do it as ducks' legs are set underneath them and it is hard to find the joints.

This recipe is for very well-done duck, it melts in the mouth. The rest in a low oven at the end, while you make the gravy, is an important part of the process. It benefits for up to half an hour; longer and it will start to dry out.

Serves 4

1 plump young duckling weighing 3½–4 lb (1.5–1.8 kg) and its giblets

1 onion

2 oranges

2 tbsp oil

1 lemon

¼ pint (150 ml) claret

½ pint (300 ml) stock

2 tsp bramble jelly or blackcurrant or redcurrant jelly

salt

Preheat the oven to 400°F (200°C, Gas 6). Put half the peeled onion and half an orange inside the duck. Rub the skin all over with the other half of the orange, prick it here and there and then coat it with oil. Put it in a roasting tin and roast in the oven for 45 minutes.

Meanwhile, pare the rind of the remaining orange and the lemon and cut it into thin strips. Blanch for 3 minutes in boiling water, and set aside.

When the duck has been cooking for 45 minutes, add the chopped giblets and the remaining half onion to the tin. Let them roast to a nice brown, about 30 minutes, then remove the duck to a serving plate and reduce the heat of the oven to 200°F (100°C, Gas ¼). Put it back to keep hot.

Skim the fat carefully off the top of the pan juices with a tablespoon, leaving only about 2 tbsp fat and all the pan juices. Add the claret and let it reduce by half over a high heat, scraping up all the caramelised juices from the tin. The giblets can now be chopped up as much as possible and put back in with the gravy with half the stock. Reduce by simmering, adding more stock and the juice from the lemon and orange as needed, and lastly the jelly and seasoning. Strain the sauce, thicken it if you like, add the julienne of orange and lemon rind and serve with the duck.

85

Braised Guinea Fowl with Chestnuts

This recipe is also extremely good made with pheasant. Major Hugh Pollard in his *Sportsman's Cookery Book* says there is a natural affinity — wild chestnuts are the pheasant's favourite food.

Serves 4

1 guinea fowl weighing 2½ lb (1.1 kg)

1–2 oz (25–50 g) streaky bacon

8 oz (225 g) button onions

8 oz (225 g) carrots

8 oz (225 g) chestnuts

1 oz (25 g) butter

1 tbsp oil

bunch of herbs (thyme, parsley, bayleaf)

salt and freshly ground pepper

2–3 tbsp red wine

¼ pint (150 ml) good chicken stock

Preheat the oven to 350°F (180°C, Gas 4). Joint the guinea fowl and cut the bacon into pieces. Peel the onions and carrots and shell the chestnuts (see below). Heat the butter and oil in a casserole. Fry the bacon and pieces of guinea fowl, browning them nicely on both sides, then remove them to a bowl. Now fry the vegetables with the guinea fowl liver and heart, cut in pieces, browning them lightly.

When they look appetising, return the bacon, add the chestnuts and put the pieces of guinea fowl back on top. Push the bouquet of herbs into the centre, season and add the wine and stock. Cover the casserole and simmer in the oven for 45 minutes. Serve with rice or potatoes.

TO PEEL CHESTNUTS

Make a slit in the shell of each chestnut. Plunge 4–5 chestnuts at a time into boiling water and boil for a minute or two. Remove with a slotted spoon, take off the shells and remove the inner skin — always a boring and fiddly job. Let some more chestnuts cook while you peel the first batch.

Braised Pigeons with Cabbage

This is based on a nineteenth-century recipe from the Red Lion Hotel, Fareham, in Hampshire. The original recipe served the birds with green peas rather than cabbage and you could do the same.

Serves 4

4 pigeons, preferably young

3 rashers bacon, rinds removed and cut up small

1½ oz (40g) butter

4 oz (100 g) mushrooms

a little flour

1 onion, chopped

¼ pint (150 ml) red wine

basil, thyme, marjoram, parsley

pinch of ground nutmeg

pinch of ground allspice

lemon rind, pared free of white pith, and a squeeze of lemon juice

salt and freshly ground pepper

1 medium Savoy or other curly green cabbage

Preheat the oven to 325°F (170°C, Gas 3).

In a heavy casserole, fry the bacon in 1 oz (25 g) butter and after a minute or two add the mushrooms. When they are lightly cooked, take them out. Dust the pigeons with flour, add a little more butter to the pan and brown the pigeons all over. When they are sealed on all sides, remove them and fry the onion until tender but not brown.

Stir the mushrooms and bacon back into the pan, put the pigeons on top and pour on the red wine. Add the herbs and spices, lemon rind and juice and season with salt and pepper. Bring to simmering point, cover the pan and braise until tender. If they are young ¾–1 hour should be enough, but older pigeons will need longer.

Meanwhile, clean the cabbage, quarter it, cut out the stalk and drop into plenty of rapidly boiling, well-salted water. Don't cover. When it is just tender, drain well and set aside.

When the pigeons are done, remove them with a slotted spoon and arrange in an oval gratin dish. Arrange the bacon and mushrooms around and on top. Skim the fat from the juices and heat the cabbage in it. Serve the pigeons with the skimmed gravy, bacon, mushrooms and juicy cabbage.

ALTERNATIVE

Leave out the mushrooms and add the cabbage, blanched for 1 minute, to the casserole with the bacon. Put the pigeons on top as before and cook pigeons and cabbage together. Serve with good mashed potatoes.

Rabbit Pie

'...I had for them, after oysters — at first course, a hash of rabbits and lamb, and a rare chine of beef — next a great dish of fowl, cost me about 30s and a tart; and then fruit and cheese. My dinner was noble and enough...'
Samuel Pepys DIARY 13 January 1663

If Samuel Pepys did not turn up his nose at rabbit, nor should we; in fact it has an excellent flavour and is very much enjoyed in the British countryside where rabbits are still all too plentiful.

Serves 4–6

1 large rabbit, preferably young

a little flour

1 tbsp butter or lard

1–2 tbsp vegetable oil

8 oz (225 g) onions, peeled and coarsely chopped

4 oz (100 g) streaky bacon, cut in pieces

$\frac{1}{2}$–$\frac{1}{4}$ tsp each dried marjoram, lemon thyme and savory

1 bayleaf

1 strip lemon rind, chopped (pare the yellow zest carefully avoiding the bitter white pith)

$\frac{1}{2}$ pint (300 ml) beef stock

a generous dash of port or red wine

salt and freshly ground pepper

4 or 5 slender carrots

1 lump of sugar

a nut of butter

8 oz (225 g) shortcrust pastry (see page 139)

1 egg yolk, for glazing

Cut the rabbit into serving-size pieces and dust them lightly in flour. Fry them, a few at a time, in butter or lard and oil, in a casserole with a heavy base. When they are a rich golden brown, fry the onions and the bacon in the same fat over a low heat.

Add the herbs, lemon rind, stock, wine or port and seasoning. Cover and simmer gently for $\frac{3}{4}$–1 hour for a tame rabbit — a wild one may take longer, according to its age.

If there seems to be too much gravy when the rabbit is tender, pour it into a small pan and simmer it, uncovered, until it is somewhat reduced. Taste for seasoning and allow to cool.

Clean the carrots, slice them about the thickness of a 1p piece and blanch for 5 minutes in boiling water with salt, a lump of sugar and a nut of butter, drain them and set them aside.

Preheat the oven to 400°F (200°C, Gas 6).

Transfer the rabbit and its juices to a large pie dish and scatter the carrots over the top. Cover with rolled out pastry, using a double thickness for the rim and taking care that it does not get stretched or it will shrink in the oven. Decorate the top with pastry leaves or rabbits and brush with egg yolk beaten with salt and a little water. Scallop or fork the edges of the pie, glaze a second time and bake at 400°F (200°C, Gas 6) for 15 minutes then cover the pie loosely with foil, turn down the heat to 350°F (180°C, Gas 4) and bake for a further 25 minutes.

Serve with good mashed potatoes.

ALTERNATIVE

Instead of carrots you could scatter over the top of the cooked rabbit a quantity of thinly sliced mushrooms cooked for a minute or two in butter.

VEGETABLES
AND SALADS

No meal is satisfying without vegetables in some shape or guise. Their colours, forms and textures are more luxurious and inspiring to look at than anything else in the kitchen, they are the culinary equivalent of flowers on the table — refreshing to the eye and a thing of beauty. I suppose that until recently English people have regarded them more as a supporting cast than actual star performers in any meal. But luckily the new health craze that has hit us all has made us more aware of their good qualities; and the new wave of cooking, so monotonous in many ways, has at least made us look at vegetables with a more imaginative eye.

Really perfect, young, fresh summer vegetables need only the simplest treatment. Brief cooking in salted water and a smothering of good fresh butter is the best thing you can do to tiny green peas like green caviare, new baby carrots, potatoes the size of marbles, asparagus, infant broad beans sweet enough to eat raw, or tiny French beans. But maturity in vegetables means they need a little extra attention — especially in autumn and winter, when old potatoes, the brassicas and fully grown root vegetables look uninspiring. Of course one can buy imported vegetables out of season to widen the range, but I rather think winter vegetables, properly cooked, go better than anything with winter food. So I have concentrated mainly on recipes for autumn and winter, and have left the summer ones to be done in typically British plain and simple style.

Tending the kitchen garden, Merton, North Devon

Harvest Festival, Atherington, North Devon

Asparagus

Asparagus is best of all served soon after it is picked, within the hour if you want perfection. In fact, Alexander Plunkett Greene's father went as far as to take a Primus stove into the kitchen garden to cook them within minutes, even seconds, of cutting them with his special asparagus knife. Where his melted butter came from is still a mystery.

Serves 6

3–4 lb (1.3–1.8 kg) asparagus

salt

6 oz (150 g) butter

Trim the tough ends off the asparagus, making the stalks all more or less the same length. Scrape away the lower scales, which may be hiding grit. Tie the stalks into as many bundles as there are people, using clean white string.

Bring a large pan of water, large enough to take the asparagus lying down, to the boil. Put in a generous amount of salt, it helps to keep the asparagus green. Lower in the bundles and boil for 15–18 minutes according to size. Test them with a thin skewer to see if they are done, then lift them out by the string. Do not put them in a colander or the tips will break off; drain them on a tilted dish with a cloth on it.

TO SERVE
Serve hot, well drained, with the string removed, on hot plates, and with a jug of drawn butter sauce: bring 2–3 tablespoons of water to the boil in a small pan. Gradually add the butter in little pieces, shaking the pan all the time. Or serve the asparagus cold, with a very good salad dressing, or mayonnaise thinned with single cream.

Green Peas

Allow 1 lb (450 g) for 2 people (or more), before shelling. Shell the peas and take note, by eating one or two raw ones, as to whether they are young and sweet or elderly and in need of help to make them taste good.

Small, young, sweet, freshly picked peas take about 5 minutes to cook in boiling salted water.

Older peas should be boiled for 15–20 minutes. Taste them after about 10 minutes and if necessary put in 1–2 lumps of sugar. A few spring or silver onions are a good addition to older peas; put them into cold salted water and bring it to the boil before you add the peas.

Serve the peas well drained and tossed in softened butter but not cooked in it. Some people put a mint leaf in the water with the peas.

A Very Good Way with Spinach

Serves 6

2 lb (900 g) young spinach

2–3 oz (50–75 g) butter

grated nutmeg

salt and freshly ground pepper

Trim and wash the spinach leaves and drain very thoroughly.

Heat the butter in a very large pan, large enough to hold all the spinach. Put in the spinach over a fairly high heat and turn it over with two large spoons until it wilts. Season it with salt, pepper and nutmeg, drain and serve.

It only takes a very few minutes, is succulent and bright green, and has the most wonderful rich and subtle flavour.

Mushroom Purée

Serves 4

1 lb (450 g) white button mushrooms

1 onion

4 oz (100 g) butter

salt and freshly ground pepper

freshly ground nutmeg

¼ pint (150 ml) double cream

Wash the mushrooms quickly in a colander under cold running water. Drain them well, trim the stalks if necessary and slice finely. Peel and chop the onion finely and soften in a wide shallow pan in 2 oz (50 g) butter, then add the sliced mushrooms. Season and cook gently, stirring them round, until all their liquid has run out and then been re-absorbed. Purée in a liquidiser or food processor.

Return the purée to the pan, add the remaining butter and cook on until the purée is rather dryish. Add the cream and more seasoning if it is needed and cook again, quite gently, until you have a nice, soft, velvety purée, pale fawn in colour.

St George's mushrooms

Mushrooms in Cream

'TO RAISE MUSHROOMS
Cover an old hot-bed three or four Inches thick, with fine Garden Mould, and cover that three or four inches thick with mouldy long muck, of an Horse Muck-Hill, or any rotten Stubble; when the Bed has lain some time thus prepared, boil any Mushrooms that are not fit for Use in Water, and throw that Water on your prepared Bed, and in a Day or two after, you will have the best small Button Mushrooms.'
Hannah Glasse THE ART OF COOKERY MADE PLAIN AND EASY 1747

This is best of all when made with country field mushrooms of your own gathering.

Serves 4

12 oz (350 g) large flat mushrooms

½ oz (15 g) butter or a little more

salt and freshly ground black pepper

a pinch or two of thyme, fresh if possible

¼ pint (150 ml) double cream

Clean the mushrooms and cut off the stalks. Heat the butter and gently fry the mushrooms, seasoning them with salt, pepper and a little thyme. When they are beginning to soften, add the cream and cook the mushrooms in it, turning them occasionally, until the cream starts to thicken and turn a rich fawn colour.

TO SERVE
Serve very hot, either on toast or with grilled steak or lamb chops.

Broad Beans in Cream with Summer Savory or Thyme

Constance Spry and Rosemary Hume in their excellent *Constance Spry Cookery Book* tell us that broad beans are delicious eaten boiled in their pods when no more than 2 inches (5 cm) long and that large beans should be eaten podded and *skinned*, a real labour of love, or turned into a purée.

I am talking about the beans in between these two stages — small but large enough to take out of their furry-lined pods. You will need a lot, as the pods weigh twice as much, or more, as the beans.

Savory is the herb traditionally associated with broad beans, but unless you have your own herb garden, it is almost impossible to find, except in a dried form.

To me, savory is very like thyme in flavour — fresh thyme is closest, so I think this would make a perfectly good substitute. Otherwise use dried savory.

Serves 4

3 lb (1.3 kg) broad beans

1–2 sprigs of savory or thyme

¼ pint (150 ml) double cream

salt and freshly ground pepper

Pod the beans, discarding any that are not perfect. Bring a large pan of well-salted water to the boil, add a sprig of savory or thyme and drop in the beans. Cook for 8 minutes then test a bean; if they are really young and tender they will not take long to cook. The longer since they were picked the tougher they will be.

Drain them well. Chop the rest of the savory or shred the leaves and flowers of the thyme. Put the herbs into the cream, season and cook gently until the cream has thickened a little, then drop in the beans and heat through.

Braised Leeks with Cream

Serves 6

2 lb (900 g) leeks

2 oz (50 g) butter

scant ¼ pint (150 ml) chicken stock

2–3 tbsp double cream

salt and a great deal of coarsely ground black pepper

Trim the leeks, removing the coarse green tops and outer layers. If necessary slit them down the centre to wash out the grit. Slice very, very thinly; they are not going to end up as chunks, but as a soft, green mass.

Melt the butter in a wide shallow pan. Soften the leeks for 5 minutes, stirring them round, then add the stock and a little salt and cook until the liquid evaporates. Add the double cream and a good quantity of pepper, either ground with a pestle and mortar or from a very coarse peppermill. Simmer until the leeks are bathed in a light creamy sauce, stirring them round to prevent them burning.

TO SERVE

Serve hot with grilled beef or lamb or with roast chicken. These leeks are also excellent with plainly cooked fish such as poached turbot or brill, or grilled sole.

Roasted Onions

These are done in almost exactly the same way as roast potatoes. They are good with roast pork, roast lamb or roast beef. You can make roast shallots in the same way (they take less time of course) and serve them with lamb chops, pork chops, lambs' kidneys or veal kidneys.

1 lb (500 g) onions

salt

1–2 oz (25–50 g) butter and a little oil or a few tablespoons of good fresh dripping from a roast chicken or a joint of pork

Preheat the oven to 375°F (190°C, Gas 5). Peel the onions, cutting off as little as possible at the root end, so that they stay whole. Put in a pan of salted water, bring to the boil and boil for 10 minutes.

Drain the onions and put into a roasting tin with the melted butter and oil or dripping. Roll them about so they are well coated, and roast them in the oven for about 45 minutes.

Prize onions, Dolton, North Devon

94

Braised Red Cabbage

Serves 6–8

a 2 lb (900 g) red cabbage

2 onions

1½ oz (40 g) butter

1–2 tbsp olive oil

2 apples, preferably russets

3 tbsp cider vinegar

3 tbsp brown muscovado sugar

dash of red wine

½ tsp each ground cinnamon and cloves

1 tsp each crushed juniper berries and coriander
    seeds

1 strip thinly pared orange rind

1 bayleaf

salt and freshly ground black pepper

Quarter the cabbage, removing the central core, and slice it into short strips. Peel and chop the onions.

Heat the butter and olive oil in a large heavy casserole and soften the onions without letting them brown. Add the cabbage and let it cook gently, stirring occasionally, for about 20 minutes. Preheat the oven to 325°F (160°C, Gas 3).

Core and roughly chop the apples and add them to the pan with the vinegar and sugar and a dash of red wine — too much liquid makes the cabbage go soft and mushy. Add all the spices and flavourings and cover the pan. Cook in the oven for 1 hour, stirring once or twice and checking to see that it does not dry out. Taste after an hour to see if the flavour still has the right balance of sweet and sharp — it tends to lose its piquancy after long cooking, in which case add more vinegar and sugar at this point.

Cook for a further 15–20 minutes until just tender. Serve drained and hot with all kinds of game or with roast pork.

Red cabbage re-heats extremely well and keeps for several days.

Buttered Cabbage

'Most people spoil garden things by over-boiling them. All things that are green should have a little crispness, for if they are over-boiled, they neither have any sweetness nor beauty.'
Hannah Glasse THE ART OF COOKERY MADE PLAIN AND EASY 1747

Serves 4–6

1 Savoy cabbage or other green cabbage

salt

2 oz (50 g) butter

coarsely ground black pepper

Bring a large pan of well-salted water to the boil.

Quarter the cabbage, remove the outer leaves and cut away the main stalk. Drop the cabbage into the fast boiling water, cover the pan to help it come back to the boil very fast, then remove the lid and turn down the heat a bit. Boil gently for 10–12 minutes, then drain really well for several minutes, cutting through the cabbage in the colander to help the water escape. It should be coarsely chopped.

Return it to the pan and add the butter in little pieces. Heat through, season with coarsely ground pepper if you like it, and if water still comes out, let it simmer gently until it has evaporated, but do not brown the cabbage, it should still be a lovely brilliant green.

95

Roast Winter Vegetables

'The quality of vegetables depends much on both the soil in which they are grown, and on the degree of care bestowed upon their culture; but if produced in ever so great perfection, their excellence will be entirely destroyed if they be badly cooked.'
Eliza Acton MODERN COOKERY FOR PRIVATE FAMILIES 1845

You can cook all or any of these winter vegetables in one great big roasting tin. They should be mellow, golden brown and delicious.

Serves 6

6–7 tbsp dripping, see method, or melted butter and oil
_____
12 small potatoes
_____
3 large parsnips
_____
12 small Jerusalem artichokes
_____
6 large carrots
_____
12 small onions
_____
3 turnips
_____
3 kohl rabi
_____
salt
_____

For the best flavour, roast the vegetables in the fat left after roasting a chicken or a piece or pork, the dripping gives a very good flavour. If however you prefer something lighter, use a mixture of olive oil and a little butter. Roast them in the oven with the joint — they take about the same time to cook as a chicken — about 1¼ hours, but they can cook for longer without coming to any harm (watch parsnips though, as they tend to burn). If you are not cooking a joint at the same time, set the oven at 375–400°F (190–200°C, Gas 5–6).

Peel all the vegetables, cut the larger ones into small chunks about the same size as the potatoes. Leave the skinned onions whole.

Bring a large pan of salted water to the boil, drop in the carrots and potatoes and cook for 5 minutes. Then add the rest of the vegetables and cook for 5 minutes more. Drain very thoroughly. Put the dripping or butter and oil in a roasting tin large enough to take all the vegetables in one layer. Heat the tin in the oven and when the fat is hot put in all the vegetables and return it to the oven. Baste the vegetables from time to time as they cook and then turn them over with a metal spoon, taking care not to break them. Add more fat if necessary.

When they are golden and tender right through when tested with a skewer, transfer the vegetables to a heated serving dish with a slotted spoon, leaving all the fat behind in the tin.

These vegetables are delicious with roast meat. An alternative way of cooking them is to do them in the tin with the joint or bird. Some people put them straight into the hot fat without any precooking at all but the parsnips and carrots can be a bit tough by this method.

Seakale

'The rib of the white beet being boiled melts, and eats like marrow . . . The roots of the red beet cut into thin slices, after being boiled, when cold, is of itself a grateful winter sallet, being mingled with oil and vinegar, salt, etc. There is also a beet growing beside the sea [sea-kale] which is the most delicate of all.'
Seventeenth century, quoted by Dorothy Hartley FOOD IN ENGLAND 1954

Allow 1 lb (450 g) seakale for 2–3 people. Wash and remove any coarse leaves and discoloured bits. Seakale should be ivory white with a pinky, yellowy, infant leaf curled up at the top of the stem. Tie it into bundles, one for each person, and cook it like asparagus (see page 91) in boiling salted water to which you have added a squeeze of lemon. Drain and cover with melted butter or with cream mixed with a little chopped tarragon. It has a delicate, somewhat nutty taste, but goes greenish and cabbagey-tasting if exposed to light for any length of time.

Puréed Swedes with Butter and Cream

Serves 4–6

2 lb (900 g) swedes

2 oz (50 g) butter

2½ fl oz (65 ml) double cream or more

salt and a generous pinch of freshly grated nutmeg

very coarsely ground black pepper (optional)

Peel the swedes and cut them into large chunks — quarters for medium swedes or smaller for larger ones — if you cut them up too small they absorb too much water. Cook in well-salted water.

When they are tender, drain them well and purée in a liquidiser or food processor.

Put the purée in a heavy pan with the butter and if they are at all watery, stir over a low heat for several minutes to evaporate some of the water. Then add the cream and season with salt and nutmeg.

Grind very coarse black pepper over the top if you like it, and finish with a big knob of butter or a swirl of cream.

ALTERNATIVE
Celeriac can be treated in the same way to produce a lovely cream-coloured purée to serve with game.

butter stamp

Scalloped Potatoes

'The allotment plots were divided into two, and one half planted with potatoes and the other half with wheat or barley. The garden was reserved for green vegetables, currant or gooseberry bushes, and a few old-fashioned flowers. Proud as they were of their celery, peas and beans, cauliflowers and marrows, and fine as were the specimens they could show of these, their potatoes were their special care, for they had to grow enough to last the year round. They grew all the old-fashioned varieties — ashleaf kidney, early rose, American rose, and the huge misshaped white elephant.'
Flora Thompson LARK RISE TO CANDLEFORD 1939

Serves 6

1 oz (25 g) butter

1 oz (25 g) flour

1 pint (550 ml) milk

salt, pepper and nutmeg

1½ lb (675 ml) potatoes

2–3 tbsp chopped parsley

1 oz (25 g) grated Cheddar cheese

a nut of butter

Make a béchamel sauce: melt the butter in a pan, stir in the flour and cook for 1–2 minutes. Away from the heat, gradually stir in the milk, then return to heat and cook, stirring, until thickened and smooth. Season well with salt, pepper and nutmeg.

Peel the potatoes and slice them thinly, either by hand, on a mandoline, or in a food processor. Butter a 12 inch (30 cm) oval gratin dish and put in a layer of potatoes. Season lightly and cover with a layer of béchamel sauce. Sprinkle with half the parsley. Repeat these layers, then finish with a layer of potatoes, a layer of béchamel and a layer of grated cheese. Dot the top with butter.

The potatoes can either be given a long slow cooking if they are to go in with a roasting joint, or a fast burst in a hot oven. The slow method will need 1 hour at 350°F (180°C, Gas 4). The fast method will need 30–40 minutes at 425°F (220°C, Gas 7). Cover loosely with foil if they look as if they are burning.

Cheese and Potato Supper

'There is no vegetable commonly cultivated in this country, we venture to assert, which is comparable in value to the potato when it is of a good sort, has been grown in a suitable soil and is properly cooked and served.'
Eliza Acton MODERN COOKERY FOR PRIVATE FAMILIES 1845

This is a sort of last resort recipe, to make when there isn't much in the larder, and you don't want to go out. It is also known as Irish Vegetable, or just Irish, Hot Pot. Soothing on its own, and good with grilled lamb cutlets.

Serves 4

2 lb (1 kg) potatoes

4 oz (100 g) Cheshire, Lancashire or Cheddar cheese

a little butter

coarse salt and freshly ground black pepper

$\frac{1}{4}$ pint (150 ml) milk

1 bayleaf

2–3 slices onion

Preheat the oven to 350°F (180°C, Gas 4).
    Peel the potatoes and slice them into rounds each $\frac{1}{8}$ inch (3 mm) thick. Grate the cheese, using the coarse side of the grater.
    Butter a 10 inch (25 cm) oval ovenproof dish and cover the bottom with a layer of sliced potatoes. Season with coarse salt and very coarsely ground pepper and cover with a layer of cheese. Repeat the operation — you should be able to make about 4 layers of potatoes. Finish with a layer of cheese. Cover the dish and bake in the oven for 30 minutes.
    Meanwhile, pour the milk into a saucepan and add the bayleaf and 2 or 3 slices of onion. Heat through gently, and keep hot to infuse. After the potato and cheese layers have baked for 30 minutes, remove the dish from the oven and strain the hot milk over them. Return the dish to the oven for a further 30–40 minutes, by which time the potatoes should have absorbed the milk and be cooked.

Earthing up potatoes, Dolton, North Devon

Game Chips

Buy the largest potatoes you can find, and allow 1 per person. Peel them as thinly as possible and slice them into rounds, again as thinly as possible, by hand or on a mandoline slicer. Put the slices into a bowl of cold water for a few minutes, then take out a handful and dry them carefully on a clean drying up cloth.

Heat a mixture of sunflower and olive oil in a deep-frying pan. Lower the basket containing a handful of dry slices of potato into the sizzling hot oil and keep the slices moving about as they fry. When they are pale golden, lift up the basket, increase the heat a little under the pan and then dip them back in until they are a rich golden brown more or less all over. Lift them out, shake well and drain on kitchen paper while you cook the next handful, turning the heat down a little to start with.

You can cook these early in the day and reheat them in the oven just before serving. They are exquisite, and perfect with partridge, pheasant or grouse. If you haven't time to make them yourself — they do take quite a lot of effort — then serve roast potatoes, never bought potato crisps.

Picking potatoes, Westacott, North Devon

100

Potato, Celery and Chive Salad

Serves 6

1½ lb (675 g) small new potatoes

3 inner sticks of celery

1 small onion

2–3 tbsp chopped chives

¼ pint (150 ml) home-made mayonnaise or rather
   more

salt and freshly ground black pepper

Scrub the potatoes in their skins and put into a pan
of boiling salted water. Bring back to the boil and
cook for 15–20 minutes. Drain, cool a little and peel
if the skins seem tough. (Peeling potatoes after they
are cooked is easier if you only take them out of the
water one at a time.)

You can either use the potatoes whole or cut them
into slices, about ¼ inch (6 mm) thick. Put them in a
bowl. Slice the celery thinly and peel and chop the
onion very finely; add to the potatoes. Mix in the
mayonnaise, adding more if necessary, as some
potatoes are quite absorbent. Taste for seasoning
and add salt and plenty of pepper. Stir in half the
chives. Transfer to a clean salad bowl and sprinkle
with the rest of the chives. Serve the salad soon
after it is made.

ALTERNATIVES
Flavour the salad with chopped mint instead of
chives. Use salad dressing instead of mayonnaise.

Champ

'MASHED POTATOES
*I had better say that what I am looking for in the
result is a creamy, almost foaming, whipped-up
pyramid of such fineness that it would be impossible
for a lump to live in it.'*
Constance Spry COME INTO THE GARDEN COOK
1942

Serves 4–6

2 lb (1 kg) potatoes

1 bunch spring onions

1 oz (25 g) butter

a little milk

salt and freshly ground pepper

Peel the potatoes and put them to boil in well-salted
water. Skin and trim the spring onions, leaving
about 1 inch (2.5 cm) of the tender part of the green
tops. Cut them across diagonally into small pieces.

Melt the butter in a shallow pan and put in the
chopped spring onions. Add enough water to cover
them and simmer until it has just evaporated and
the onions are tender and bathed in a velvety, pale
green, creamy liquid.

When the potatoes are tender, drain and mash
them thoroughly over a low heat; add enough milk
to make a soft purée, and give them a really good
beating. Add the onions and stir them in; taste for
seasoning. Serve piping hot.

Sorrel Salad

Serves 4

rich salad dressing (see page 147)

2 crisp lettuces such as Buttercrunch, with nice yellow hearts

3 handfuls of young sorrel leaves

3 hard-boiled eggs

Put the salad dressing in the bottom of the salad bowl. Put the salad servers side by side, ends crossed, in the bowl, so that they slightly cover the dressing — this stops the salad from going soggy while it sits and waits for its moment to come.

Throw away all the outer leaves of lettuce, don't keep any that are coarse or dark-coloured. Separate the inner leaves and put them into the salad bowl, on top of the salad servers. Put the sorrel on top.

Chop the hard-boiled eggs very coarsely and put them on top of this. Toss the salad really well at the last moment. It is very delicious with cold salmon or after any sort of fish.

Summer Salad with Flowers

'Why do not our modern cooks decorate our salads with strewings of rose-petals, violets, primroses, gillyflowers, cowslips and flowers of elder, orange, rosemary, red sage, angelica, nasturtium, wild thyme, bugloss and marigold?'
Eleanour Sinclair Rohde A GARDEN OF HERBS

I agree with her, and very much like the sound of the salad described below, with borage and nasturtium flowers.

'One of the nicest salads I ever tasted was served at an alfresco supper after a school treat. When the last child and mother had been safely stowed in the lorry that was to take them back to the village, we turned with the sound of singing in our ears back to the old Tudor house, cosily nestling high up on the hills in a protected position. The meal was served on an old Cromwellian table, in the middle of which stood a large bowl filled with salad. It was composed of all kinds of cold vegetables that had been specially cooked and mixed in the forenoon. Green peas, young and tender, were the chief ingredients; but there were many surprises in the bowl — a few mushrooms, French beans, very young carrots, asparagus tips, some artichoke bottoms etc. These had all been soaked in a rich mayonnaise, and then our clever hostess had garnished the whole with two or three lettuce leaves, young and crisp, nasturtium flowers and a few blossoms of bright blue borage. Tomatoes, sliced and dressed, were served separately . . . The salad conceived and served on such generous and aesthetic lines, was undoubtedly the dish everyone remembered.'
Dorothy Allhusen A BOOK OF SCENTS AND DISHES 1926

To make a salad of 'generous and aesthetic lines', it is highly important to keep the vegetables whole or in very large quarters; once you have started cutting them into little pieces you will end up with nothing more or less than a mean and boring Russian salad.

Lamb's Lettuce and Beetroot Salad

'In Health if Salad Herbs you can't endure,
Sick, you'll desire them or for Food or Cure.'
OLD ENGLISH PROVERB

In the winter this is one of the most excellent and well-flavoured salads you can make. If you grow lamb's lettuce this is the best way to eat it.

Serves 6

8 oz (225 g) lamb's lettuce (also known as corn salad)

2 beetroots, cooked without vinegar (4 oz/100 g each, the large ones have less flavour)

salad dressing (see page 146)

Wash the lamb's lettuce in a large basin of cold water, shaking each little bunch of leaves about in the water to get the grit out. Nip off the root with your finger- and thumbnails and drain the leaves in a colander. Then shake gently but thoroughly in a cloth or salad shaker. Transfer the lamb's lettuce to a white salad bowl.

Skin the beetroots, cut them in quarters and then slice thickly. Scatter the pieces over the top of the lamb's lettuce.

Dress with a well-flavoured, thick dressing at the table; this is extremely good with roast lamb or beef, or with game.

Salad of Watercress, Chicory and Hazelnuts

'Such things as lettuce and watercress were washed in three waters [by Laura's mother], instead of giving them the dip and shake considered sufficient by most people. Watercress had almost to be washed away, because of the story of the man who had swallowed a tadpole which had grown to a full-sized frog in his stomach. There was an abundance of watercress to be had for the picking, and a good deal of it was eaten in the spring, before it got tough and people got tired of it. Perhaps they owed much of their good health to such food.'
Flora Thompson LARK RISE TO CANDLEFORD 1939

Serves 6

2 bunches of nice, large-leaved watercress

3 heads of chicory

1½ oz (40 g) hazelnuts, preferably fresh

salad dressing (see page 146)

Wash the watercress and remove the hairy stalks and any dead or badly damaged leaves. Shake it dry in a cloth.

Remove the outside leaves from the chicory and slice lengthwise into quarters and then into eighths. Slice the hazelnuts downwards into three or four little round slices and roast them lightly in a heavy frying pan until they are golden brown.

Arrange the chicory sticking up all the way round the salad bowl and put the watercress in the middle. Scatter the nuts on top of the watercress.

TO SERVE
Pour on the dressing at the last moment before serving and turn the salad in it until it is thoroughly coated.

103

PUDDINGS
AND DESSERTS

We have a great tradition of wonderful puddings in Britain. First and foremost are the gilded aromatic pies — apple or quince, coloured red or golden with caramel and scented with cloves: these have been among the great British dishes since medieval times. In those days people chewed cloves to sweeten their breath (and prevent toothache), so it was a compliment to the beloved to tell her that her breath was 'like the steam of apple pies'. I know the particular aroma; when you bake a really well-spiced pie, the warm breath that comes puffing out is one of life's most pleasant experiences.

With pies go melting crumbles and tarts, which can be filled with all sorts of fruit, or jam or marmalade. Then come the puddings, boiled in a basin or cloth, often made with suet and sadly unfashionable today: suet is no worse for you than butter and cream so there is no need to worry if you eat it infrequently.

A very different category of puddings, and often just as rich, is that of whips, creams, syllabubs, and fools. These were wildly popular in the eighteenth century and are irresistible in the summer.

Then there are milk puddings; and finally delicate rainbow-coloured sorbets and ice-creams. These must have been something of a miracle in the days when ice came from brick ice-houses buried deep in the woods. But now we all have refrigerators, or better still sorbet-makers, which make the whole thing perfectly simple.

Apples from the orchard at Lower Langham Farm, North Devon

104

Light Christmas Pudding

*'On the morning of the harvest home dinner
everybody prepared themselves for a tremendous
feast, some to the extent of going without breakfast,
that the appetite might not be impaired. And what
a feast it was! Such a bustling in the farmhouse
kitchen for days beforehand; such boiling of hams
and roasting of sirloins; such a stacking of plum
pudding made by the Christmas recipe; such a
tapping of eighteen-gallon casks and baking of plum
loaves would astonish those accustomed to the
appetites of today.'*
Flora Thompson LARK RISE TO CANDLEFORD 1939

Make this pudding a few days before Christmas or
on Christmas Eve if you like, it needs no maturing.
First, and highly important, is the shopping. To
make a really good pudding you must go to the
healthfood shop and buy proper golden Demerara
sugar, untreated sun-dried muscatels or jumbo
raisins — these are the sticky ones, not the ones you
eat with almonds — and untreated sun-dried sultanas. Do not buy currants — you don't need them
for this pudding. Find an old-fashioned grocer who
sells whole pieces of candied orange, lemon and
citron peel, and buy some of each — do not buy cut
peel or, worse still, those boxes of mixed dried fruit.
It is just not good enough for this pudding.

You will need ground almonds — I make them
myself, buying whole skinned almonds and grinding
them a bit coarser than the ones you buy already
ground. A food processor does this very well.

On the day you are going to make the pudding,
buy or make a loaf of wholemeal bread that has air
in it — you must not use a brick-like loaf or the
breadcrumbs will not be as light as they should be.
You will also need some free-range eggs and a nice
lemon (scrub the skin with a little vinegar to remove
any preservative from the outside), some Normandy
butter, a whole nutmeg, ground cinnamon and
mixed spice, brandy and milk.

Serves 6–8

2 oz (50 g) whole pieces of candied peel

3 oz (75 g) fine fresh wholemeal bread without
crusts

8 oz (225 g) large seedless raisins

8 oz (225 g) sultanas

3 oz (75 g) ground almonds

4 oz (100 g) Demerara sugar

pinch of sea salt

3 oz (75 g) softened unsalted butter

juice and grated rind of ½ large or 1 small lemon

2 eggs

3 tbsp brandy

1 tbsp milk

¼ tsp freshly grated nutmeg

½ tsp ground cinnamon

½ tsp mixed spice

Pour boiling water over the candied peel and let it
soak for 3–4 minutes, then drain and cut into slivers.
Make fine breadcrumbs with the wholemeal bread.
Mix together the large raisins, separated from each
other with your fingers if necessary, candied peel,
ground almonds, breadcrumbs, Demerara sugar and
salt. Stir in the butter or rub it into the dry
ingredients with the fingertips, until it is well mixed
in. Add the grated lemon rind and juice.

Beat together the eggs, brandy and milk,
whisking them well, then add them to the bowl and
mix in. Lastly, add the spices, using less or more
according to your own taste. Let everyone stir the
pudding for good luck, then put the mixture into a
buttered 1¾ pint (1 litre) pudding basin. Push in
silver charms or a silver sixpence.

Place a disc of buttered greaseproof paper on top
of the mixture, cover the top loosely with a round of
kitchen foil and tie it on with a piece of string,
making a handle across the top to lift the pudding.
Steam for 4 hours.

TO SERVE

On Christmas Day itself steam the pudding for
1 hour and serve with light brandy sauce (see page
155). Don't forget to pour heated brandy over the
top and set it alight as the pudding makes its grand
entrance at the Christmas dinner table.

Snapdragons

A Christmas game

1 lb (450 g) really good juicy muscatel raisins

8 oz (225 g) unblanched almonds

2½ fl oz (60 ml) brandy or more (or much more)

Put the muscatels and almonds on a dish and heat in a low oven for a few minutes. Heat the brandy in a small pan. Put the dish of warm almonds and raisins on the table, pour on the brandy and light it. The idea is to snatch them out of the blue flames, but they are still wonderfully good after the flames have gone out. This can also be done with whole peeled and skinned chestnuts.

Frosted Grapes

It takes time to make a large dish of frosted grapes but it is worth it. They will keep for two days.

about 4 oz (100 g) caster sugar

2 egg whites

pinch of salt

a fine bunch of black grapes

Put the caster sugar on a plate. Lightly fork the egg whites and salt together but do not whisk. Coat the grapes with the egg whites and then put them on the plate of sugar and sprinkle sugar thickly all over them with a spoon. Shake well and leave to dry.

Serve the grapes piled on a stand with fresh vine leaves underneath.

Lighting the candles on the Christmas tree, Woolridge, North Devon

Welsh Amber Pudding

'There was also Cornish cream and honey, and the butter was as golden as if King Midas had had a finger in putting up the pats.'
Richard Dehan MAIDS IN A MARKET GARDEN

The original recipe from Lady Sarah Lindsay's book — *Choice Recipes*, written in 1883 — used noyeau gin flavoured with bitter almond or apricot kernels. If you can obtain noyeau, amaretto or ratafia, use this instead of brandy to obtain the authentic flavour, but the pudding is excellent made with cognac or even whisky.

Serves 4–6

2 eggs

3 egg yolks

grated rind of 1 orange and 1 lemon

1 tbsp cognac

3 oz (75 g) sugar

4 oz (100 g) butter, melted

9½ inch (24 cm) shortcrust flan case, pre-baked blind (see page 134)

Preheat the oven to 325°F (170°C, Gas 3).
   Beat the eggs, egg yolks, grated rinds, cognac and sugar together in a bowl, add the melted butter and whisk together. Pour the mixture into the flan case and bake for 30 minutes. The filling will bubble and become deliciously crusted and flecked with golden patches.

TO SERVE
Let the flan rest for 10–15 minutes before cutting it, then serve warm with cream. The tart should be tender, melting and translucent.

Eighteenth-century Syllabub

'Take three pints of the thickest and sweetest cream you can get, a pint of rhenish [wine], half a pint of sack [sherry], three lemons, near a pound of double-refined sugar, beat and sift the sugar and put it to your cream, grate off the yellow rind of three lemons, put that in and squeeze the juice of three lemons into your wine; put that to your cream, beat all together with a spoon, and fill your glasses.'
Hannah Glasse THE COMPLEAT CONFECTIONER 1760

Kent Syllabub

Make this in the morning if it is for lunch, in the afternoon if for dinner. If you keep it longer than an hour or two it tastes better than ever but it eventually tends to separate a little at the bottom. If you do want to keep it, put it in a shallow dish in the coldest part of the refrigerator.

Serves 4–6

4 egg whites

2 tbsp caster sugar

½ pint (300 ml) double cream

grated rind and juice of 1 lemon

about 4 fl oz (100 ml) sweet white wine, Vouvray or Barsac

Whisk the egg whites until they are a firm snow, then whisk in the sugar 1 tbsp at a time. The meringue should be smooth, shiny and thick.
   Whip the cream until it is beginning to thicken,

Bideford Pannier Market, North Devon

then slowly add the lemon rind and juice, whisking all the time. Then whisk in the wine. The mixture should be thick, soft and smooth, but still pourable. Whisk the cream gradually into the meringue.

Spoon the light, billowy mixture into champagne flutes or other pretty glasses and chill for 1 hour before serving.

Worcestershire Syllabub

'A WORCESTERSHIRE SYLLABUB
If it be in the field, only milk the Cow into the Cyder
... and so drink it.'
R. Bradley THE COUNTRY HOUSEWIFE AND LADY'S DIRECTOR 1732

A Trifle

'A TRIFLE

Take a pint of cream and boil it, when it's almost cold, sweeten it to your taste, and put it in the bason you use it in, and put to it a spoonful of Rennet, let it stand till it comes like a cheese; You may perfume it or put in orange flower water. Whip cream to a froth and lay over it.'

THE RECEIPT BOOK OF ELIZABETH RAPER
1756–70

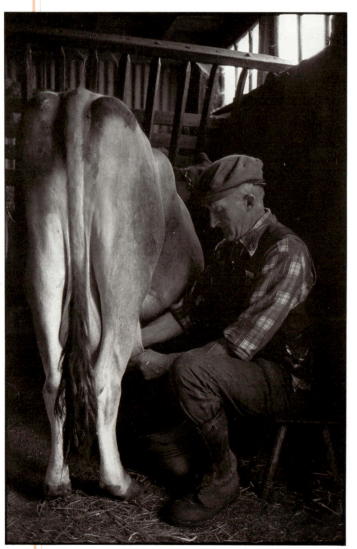

Gordon Sanders milking, Ashreigney, North Devon

The prettiest possible decoration for a trifle must be that suggested by Mrs Copley in her *Domestic Cookery* of 1845: 'Stick here and there a delicate flower. Be careful to choose only such as are innocent: violets, heart's ease, polyanthus, primrose, cowslip, geranium, myrtle, verbena, jasmine, stock, gilliflower (pink) and small roses. This will afford a variety and some of them be in season at most times of the year. The trifle is better for being made the day before, but not garnished till the moment of serving.'

Serves 6

1 plain sponge cake

4 tbsp strawberry or raspberry jam (see page 153) or redcurrant jelly (see page 151)

4 fl oz (100 ml) sweet white wine

2 tbsp brandy

a little nutmeg

2 oz (50 g) blanched almonds

1 pint (550 ml) best home-made custard (see page 155)

½ pint (300 ml) double cream, whipped and flavoured with sugar, grated lemon rind and a little brandy

a few fresh flowers for decoration

Put the plain sponge cake, spread with jam and cut in pieces, in a trifle dish; a glass bowl is traditional. Pour on the white wine and brandy and let it soak in. Grate a little nutmeg over the top and stick the pieces with split blanched almonds. Pour on the warm custard and leave it to set and cool.

Lastly cover the top with whipped cream, and decorate it with flowers.

ALTERNATIVE

Make a marmalade trifle using good home-made orange marmalade (page 153) instead of jam or redcurrant jelly.

Sussex Pond Pudding

Serves 4–6

6 oz (175 g) self-raising flour

2 oz (50 g) sugar

3 oz (75 g) suet

pinch of salt

½ beaten egg

water to mix

FILLING

1 lemon

3 oz (75 g) caster sugar

3 oz (75 g) butter

Mix the flour, sugar, suet and salt in a bowl, add the beaten egg and a few tablespoons of water and mix to a light dough. Roll it out and use to line a buttered 1½ pint (850 ml) pudding basin.

Grate the lemon rind and mix it together with the sugar and butter in a bowl. Work to a smooth paste. Now peel all the pith from the lemon and slice it thinly. Put the butter mixture and slices of lemon into the middle of the suet crust, alternating each slice of lemon with some of the mixture. Fold the paste over the top like an apple dumpling.

Cover the basin with a round of buttered foil, tie it in place with string and steam in a covered pan of boiling water which comes two thirds of the way up the sides of the basin for 2½ hours, topping up the water from time to time.

TO SERVE

Serve turned out, piping hot, and with cream or custard (page 155). When you cut the pudding you will find a succulent lemon 'pond' inside. This is delicious for lunch on a cold wintry day.

Bread and Butter Pudding

A richer version of this pudding can be made, such as was served at the Dorchester in London to a party of Britain's top food writers and 3-star French chefs. They thought it was sublime. Substitute single cream for the milk, and add a handful of sultanas soaked in brandy.

Serves 4

6 small slices day old bread, crusts cut off

butter for the bread

1 oz (25 g) sultanas

2 eggs

½ pint (300 ml) milk

2–3 tbsp double cream

4 tsp sugar or 3 tsp sugar and 1 tsp vanilla sugar

a grating of nutmeg

The oven should be fairly low otherwise the custardy part, which should be creamy and delicate, will separate. Preheat it to 325°F (170°C, Gas 3).

Butter the slices of bread. Put 3 slices in a 10 inch (25 cm) pie dish, scatter on the sultanas and put the remaining three slices on top. Heat the milk.

Beat the eggs, hot milk, cream and sugar together and pour over the bread and butter. Allow to soak for 15 minutes then bake, covered, for 20 minutes.

Uncover the pudding, sprinkle with sugar and nutmeg and bake for another 20–25 minutes until just set.

Bread from Bert Foxwell's bakery, Churchingford, Taunton, Somerset

111

Steamed Ginger Pudding

I invented this pudding, a mixture of treacle sponge and a ginger pudding from the nineteenth century, because I so much like the gooey syrupy top on a treacle pudding. If you don't want to serve it with cream, heat some of the syrup from the ginger jar with a couple of pieces of ginger, finely chopped, in it and serve it as a sauce.

Serves 4–6

FOR THE SYRUP

2 oz (50 g) butter

2 oz (50 g) sugar

2 generous tbsp syrup from a jar of preserved ginger

FOR THE PUDDING

6 oz (175 g) self-raising flour

4 oz (100 g) prepared suet

4 oz (100 g) soft brown sugar

1 tsp ground ginger

pinch of salt

6 fl oz (175 ml) milk

5–6 pieces preserved ginger in syrup, chopped

Put the butter, sugar and ginger syrup into a small saucepan and stir them together until lightly coloured to a pale, creamy, toffee colour. Pour the mixture into a buttered pudding basin of 1½ pints (850 ml) capacity.

Mix the flour, suet, sugar, ground ginger and salt together in a bowl and stir in enough milk to give a soft, dropping consistency. Add the chopped preserved ginger. Spoon the mixture into the basin on top of the ginger syrup. Tie kitchen foil, buttered on the inside, over the top, crossing the string over the middle to make a handle.

Place the bowl in a large saucepan and add enough boiling water to come halfway up the sides. Cover the pan and steam at a steady rolling boil for 3 hours, adding more boiling water as necessary to keep up the level.

TO SERVE

Take the pudding out of the water, run a spatula quickly round the inside and turn it upside down over a deep plate or dish. It should slide out neatly. Spoon over any ginger syrup left in the bottom of the basin and serve the pudding very hot, with a jug of cream.

Berkshire Baked Custard

'They were the less restful cows that were stalled. Those that would stand still of their own will were milked in the middle of the yard, where many of such better behaved ones stood waiting now — all prime milchers, such as were seldom seen out of this valley, and not always within it; nourished by the succulent feed which the water-meads supplied at this prime season of the year. Those of them that were spotted with white reflected the sunshine in dazling brilliancy, and the polished brass knobs on their horns glittered with something of military display. Their large-veined udders hung ponderous as sandbags, the teats sticking out like the legs of a gipsy's crock; and as each animal lingered for her turn to arrive the milk oozed forth and fell in drops on the ground.'
Thomas Hardy TESS OF THE D'URBERVILLES 1891

Serves 6

1½ pints (850 ml) creamy milk

grated rind of 1 lemon, or 1 vanilla pod

3–4 oz (75–100 g) caster sugar

1 tbsp brandy

4 eggs

nutmeg

Preheat the oven to 325°F (160°C, Gas 3). Heat the milk, lemon rind or vanilla pod, sugar and brandy to boiling point, then remove from the heat.

Beat the eggs lightly without making them froth — it is best to use a fork for this rather than a whisk, or the top of the custard will be bubbly and look as if

Cows eating thistleheads, Dolton, North Devon

it is curdled. Pour the hot, but not boiling, milk on to the eggs, stirring all the time with a wooden spoon. Strain through a wire sieve into a 2 pint (1.1 litre) pie dish.

Sprinkle the top with grated nutmeg (or coriander or cinnamon) and bake for 50–60 minutes, until set but still tender and wobbly.

TO SERVE
Baked custard is lovely on its own or with a dish of stewed greengages or plums, or poached peaches or pears. Eat it sprinkled with sugar.

TO MAKE A CUSTARD PIE
Use the same custard to make a proper custard pie — the sort that Laurel and Hardy used to throw at each other before the invention of shaving cream.

See page 139 for instructions for making and precooking the crust, and add the custard at the same time as you would add any other sort of filling. Sprinkle the top with nutmeg and bake at 325°F (160°C, Gas 3) for 40–50 minutes.

Milk boiler from *The Ironmonger* 28 June 1913

Compôte of Pears

Serves 6

6 large, firm, perfect Conference pears, or other nice English eating pears

SYRUP

10 oz (300 g) sugar

1 vanilla pod, or 1 tbsp vanilla sugar

thinly pared rind of ½ lemon

juice of a whole lemon

Simmer all the syrup ingredients together with 3 pints (1.7 litres) water for half an hour.

Peel the pears thinly with a stainess steel knife; they look prettier if you leave their stalks on. As each is peeled, slip it into the simmering syrup. Poach them gently for 30–40 minutes, turning them over once or twice. Leave to cool in their liquid and serve drained and arranged in a dish, with lightly whipped cream and a few crystallised violets.

VARIATION

Peaches can be poached in the same syrup. Skin them first, pouring boiling water over them so that the skins will slip off easily. Cook for 20–30 minutes. Serve cool, piled in a beautiful dish, with a jug of cream. They have the most beautiful flavour, a pretty pink flush on the side and a delicious succulence; white peaches are even more delicate than the more ordinary yellow ones.

Caledonian Cream with Orange Salad

'ORANGES IN SUGAR, A PRETTY LITTLE DISH
Skin four or five oranges, carefully remove all the scurf and thready parts. Cut them in round slices and dress them in a small glass dish in hot syrup. Garnish with sprigs of myrtle.'
Mistress Margaret Dods THE COOK AND HOUSEWIVES' MANUAL 1829

Serves 4–6

1 heaped tbsp home-made marmalade

1 tbsp brandy

juice of ½ lemon

½ pint (300 ml) double cream

2–3 tsp caster sugar

a few unsalted pistachio nuts

1 oz (25 g) blanched almonds

FOR THE ORANGE SALAD

6 oranges

caster sugar

Put the marmalade in a bowl and chop the peel into small pieces. Mix it with the brandy and lemon juice.

Whisk the cream until it just holds its shape, stir in the marmalade mixture and then whisk in enough sugar to sweeten it lightly. Pile the whipped cream into a bowl.

Pour boiling water on the pistachio nuts, leave for a few minutes and then skin them. Cut the almonds and pistachio nuts in halves lengthwise and stick them all over the top of the cream like a hedgehog.

ORANGE SALAD

First peel the oranges with a very sharp stainless steel knife, cutting away all the pith and leaving the orange 'nude'. Now either cut across into round slices or cut carefully down the sides of the membranes that divide the orange into segments. Do this over a bowl to collect the juice. Each segment will come away neatly, leaving only the membrane behind. Squeeze the membranes to extract all the remaining juice and sprinkle the oranges with sugar. Leave to soak in their own juice.

TO SERVE

Serve the salad with the Caledonian cream as an accompaniment.

Rhubarb Fool

'And now the dairy claims her choicest care,
And half her household find employment there:
Slow rolls the churn, its load of clogging cream
At once forgoes its quality and name;
From knotty particles first floating wide,
Congealing butter's dash'd from side to side;
Streams of new milk through flowing coolers stray,
And snow-white curds abound, and wholesome
whey.'
  Robert Bloomfield (1766–1823) 'The Farmer's Boy'

Serves 4–6

1 lb (450 g) rhubarb

9 oz (250 g) sugar

½ pint (300 ml) double cream

Wash the rhubarb and trim off the ends and the
leaves. Cut it into 1 inch (2.5 cm) pieces and put
them in a pan with 2 tbsp water and 2 tbsp of the
sugar. Heat very slowly, covered, so that the
rhubarb softens and thins to a purée. Then add the
remaining sugar and cook uncovered until the purée
is thick but soft and a delicate shade of pink. It must
not be wet and sloshy. Let it get quite cool.
  Whip the cream with 2 tbsp iced water, whisking
carefully as it thickens; stop while it is still soft or
you may end up with butter, or at best a rather
grainy-textured fool.
  Fold the rhubarb purée into the cream, pour it
into a serving dish and chill. Serve, if you like, with a
little extra cream.
  When making gooseberry, strawberry, raspberry
or rhubarb fool, I do not fold in the fruit too
thoroughly; it is prettier and fresher looking to have
a rather rough and ready texture, prettily marbled
and streaked with cream.
  Gooseberry fool can be made in the same way as
rhubarb, and is less inclined to be wet, so needs less
cooking. Raspberries and strawberries are lightly
crushed, sweetened and folded into the whipped
cream fresh and raw.

Greengage Crumble

'"It's very strong," said Miss Poole, as she put down
her empty glass, "I do believe there's spirit in it."
  "Only a little drop — just necessary to make it
keep," said Miss Barker, "You know we put
brandy-pepper over our preserves to make them
keep. I often feel tipsy myself from eating damson
tart".'
  Mrs Gaskell CRANFORD 1853

Greengage crumble is a variation on the lovely old
favourite lunch-time pudding, apple, or blackberry
and apple, crumble, classic dishes that children love.
They are made in exactly the same way as greengage crumble, but instead of whisky use 2–3 tsp
water or apple juice to start the fruit cooking and
producing its own juices. In apple crumble a good
dose of cinnamon in the crumbled top gives it a nice
flavour. You can use soft brown sugar instead of
caster if you prefer.

Serves 6

2 lb (900 g) greengages

6 oz (175 g) caster sugar

4 tsp whisky

3 oz (75 g) flour

4 oz (100 g) butter

salt

Preheat the oven to 375°F (190°C, Gas 5).
  Stone the greengages and put them into an oval
pie dish. Sprinkle them with 2 oz (50 g) sugar, 2 tsp
whisky and 2–3 tbsp water.
  Put the flour, remaining sugar, butter and pinch
of salt into a bowl. Sprinkle with 2 tsp whisky. Cut
the butter into the flour mixture with a knife and
then rub it in with your fingertips. The mixture
should be rough and rather sticky. Spread it over the
greengages as well as you can but leave it rough, do
not smooth it down.
  Cook in the oven for 1 hour until golden on top.
Serve hot with cream or custard (page 155).

Apple Pie

'Of all the delicates which Britons try
To please the palate or delight the eye,
Of all the sev'ral kinds of sumptuous fare,
There is none that can with apple pie compare.

Ranged in thick order let your quinces lie,
They give a charming relish to the Pie.
If you are wise you'll not brown sugar slight,
The browner (if I form my judgment right)
A deep vermilion tincture will dispense,
And make your Pippin redder than the Quince.'
William King THE ART OF COOKERY 1708

Serves 6

2½ lb (1.1 kg) cooking apples

juice of ½ lemon

3 oz (75 g) caster or brown sugar

3 cloves

generous pinch of freshly pounded cinnamon stick
  (or ground cinnamon)

rough puff pastry (see page 138) made with 6 oz
  (175 g) flour

beaten egg, for the glaze

caster sugar

Peel, quarter and core the apples, and cut them into slices. Sprinkle them with lemon juice and toss them so they are evenly coated. Put them into a 9 inch (23 cm) deep oval pie dish with a pie funnel in the middle, and sprinkle with sugar. Scatter on the spices. The pie should be neither too sweet nor too sour. If the apples seem particularly unripe, hard or sour add an extra 1 oz (25 g) sugar.

Preheat the oven to 400°F (200°C, Gas 6). Roll out the pastry. Put a rim of pastry onto the edge of the pie dish, brushing the dish with egg glaze to make it stick. Glaze the pastry rim and lift the remaining pastry into place. Trim and scallop the pie and decorate with leaves. Brush it with egg glaze.

Bake for 10–15 minutes, until the pastry has set, and then lower the heat to 325°F (160°C, Gas 3) and bake for a further 25–30 minutes or more. Take it out of the oven and sprinkle the top with caster sugar.

TO SERVE
Serve with double cream, not whipped, and a bowl of caster sugar on the table.

Apple store, Burford, Oxfordshire

Apple picking, Langham, North Devon

Gathering blackberries

Bramble Pie

Serves 4

shortcrust pastry made with 8 oz (225 g) flour (see page 139)

6 oz (175 g) blackberries

1 medium sized dessert apple, peeled, cored and thinly sliced

3 oz (75 g) sugar

1 dessertspoon plain flour

good pinch ground cinnamon

good pinch ground allspice

4 or 5 cloves

juice of $\frac{1}{2}$ orange

1 egg white

a little sugar for finishing

Butter an 8–9 inch (20–23 cm) pie plate. Roll out half the pastry $\frac{1}{8}$ inch (3 mm) thick (keep the rest in the fridge) and line the plate, trimming the edges with a sharp knife.

Put the blackberries and apple into the middle. Mix the sugar, flour and spices and sprinkle them over the top. Pour on the orange juice and cover with the remaining pastry, rolled out to the same thickness. Trim the edges and crimp them. Make a hole in the centre. Brush the top with very lightly beaten egg white. Sprinkle with sugar and bake at 425°F (220°C, Gas 7) for 15 minutes and then at 350°F (180°C, Gas 4) for a further 15–20 minutes till the pie is well risen and golden.

Melons with Frosted Redcurrants

If you have any chance of obtaining white currants they look very beautiful in a pale green melon such as Ogen. When redcurrants are out of season small seedless grapes can be frosted in the same way.

Serves 6

3 small Charentais melons

salt

1–2 egg whites

12 oz (350 g) redcurrants on their stalks

caster sugar

a few fresh mint leaves

Chill the melons.

Add a small pinch of salt to the egg whites. Break them up with a fork but do not beat them; you do not want bubbles and froth.

Pick up the bunches of currants by the stalks, one at a time, and dip them into the egg white. Shake them well so they are lightly coated, not too gooey, and then dip and turn them in the sugar. Lay them, well separated, on a wire rack to dry. Treat the mint leaves by coating them thinly with egg white with the back of a teaspoon and then dipping and drying them in the same way.

Serve the melons, chilled, halved and seeded, with the centres full of redcurrants and a mint leaf on each.

Summer Pudding

Summer pudding would follow well after a chicken salad on a hot day; it can be made with any soft fruit, but raspberries and red or blackcurrants are the most traditional. Make it a day ahead and cook the fruit lightly with sugar so that there is plenty of juice to soak the bread. A similar pudding is called Paradise Pudding. Sweet stewed fruit is alternated with layers of bread soaked in milk, ending with a layer of bread, in a glass bowl. The pudding is covered with a blanket of whipped cream and chilled for several hours.

Summer pudding should be a beautiful deep carmine colour. If the fruit is very juicy strain off some of the juice, or it will make the bread too wet and it will crumble. There should be just enough to colour it right through. Serve any extra juice separately, or pour it round the pudding at the last minute.

Serves 6

1 lb (450 g) raspberries

8 oz (225 g) sugar

1 lb (450 g) blackcurrants or redcurrants or 8 oz (225 g) of each

3 oz (75 g) caster sugar

8 slices white bread, crusts removed

Make this the day before so that the bread becomes thoroughly steeped in the juices.

Cook the raspberries briefly with the sugar until their juice flows. Soften the blackcurrants (and redcurrants if you have them) separately, taking care to let them cook slowly with a little sugar so that they retain their shape. Line a 2 pint (1.1 litre) pudding basin with the slices of bread, cutting them into shapes that fit together neatly round the bottom and sides. Fill first with redcurrants then with blackcurrants — or with blackcurrants only — and follow with a generous layer of raspberries. Enclose the fruit carefully with more trimmed slices of bread and cover with a plate. Weight the plate with a full bottle or jar (do not use a metal weight in case this comes in contact with the juices from the fruit and imparts a metallic flavour).

Leave in a cool place overnight — not the refrigerator.

TO SERVE

Turn the pudding carefully out of the basin on to a dish, decorate with bunches of fresh redcurrants and leaves, and serve with thick cream.

Exotic Fruit Salad

'And still she slept an azure-lidded sleep
In blanched linen, smooth and lavendered,
While he from forth the closet brought a heap
Of candied apple, quince and plum and gourd;
With jellies soother than the creamy curd,
And lucent syrops, tinct with cinnamon;
Manna and Dates, in argosy transferred
From Fez; and spiced dainties, every one,
From silken Samarcand to cedared Lebanon.

These delicates he heaped with glowing hand
On golden dishes and in baskets bright
Of wreathed silver;'
 John Keats (1795–1821) 'The Eve of St Agnes'

This fruit salad is not made with a syrup as it should have a sorbet-like freshness. It makes a very good end to a rich meal. It can be made the day before.

Serves 6

2 pink grapefruit (must be pink)
2 oranges
3 passion fruit
1 pineapple
1 mango
1 pomegranate
1 medium bunch black grapes
juice of 1 lemon
3–4 tbsp caster sugar, or more or less to taste
2 tbsp Kirsch or rosewater

Cut the peel and pith right away from the grapefruit, holding them over a bowl. Cut out the segments sliding the knife flat against the divisions between the segments. Squeeze the remaining membranes and pith in your hand to extract the juice. Remove the orange segments in the same way and place in the bowl with the grapefruit segments.

Peel, core and slice the pineapple. Cut the pineapple and mango into pieces the same size and shape as the orange segments, dropping them into the bowl and mixing them with the grapefruit and orange juices to keep their colour fresh. Halve the passion fruit and scoop the insides into the bowl.

Cut the pomegranate in half and remove the ruby-coloured seeds carefully, taking care not to leave any bitter yellow skin attached. Halve the grapes and remove their pips.

Mix everything together lightly, squeeze on the lemon juice and sprinkle with sugar. Leave to soak in its own juice. Add the Kirsch or rosewater just before serving.

VARIATIONS

You could also add melon, pears, ripe red plums, paw-paws, guavas and fresh strawberries (put these in at the last minute).

Another way of presenting a fruit salad is to arrange each kind of fruit round the bowl separately so that you have patches of different colours, pink grapefruit next to mango, next to the strawberries and so on. Scatter pomegranate seeds over the top.

A SIMPLER VERSION
but still very good, fresh and pretty.

2 pink grapefruit
2–3 large oranges
1 ripe mango
1 small pineapple
2 peaches, skinned
2–3 tbsp caster sugar

Purple Fruit Salad

Serves 6

1 lb (450 g) blackberries

juice of 1 lemon

3–4 tbsp sugar

6 figs

8 oz (225 g) raspberries

Put the blackberries in a bowl, sprinkle them with some of the lemon juice and sugar.

Cut the figs into quarters lengthwise and arrange them, stalks inwards, on top of the blackberries. Sprinkle with more lemon juice and sugar. Finish with the raspberries and a layer of lemon and sugar.

Chill for at least a couple of hours before serving to allow time for the juices to collect.

Poached Peaches in Champagne

Serves 6

8 oz (225 g) sugar

6 large ripe peaches

juice of 1 lemon

1 vanilla pod, split

1 glass champagne

Make a syrup by dissolving the sugar in 1 pint (550 ml) water and boiling it for 5 minutes.

Pour boiling water over the peaches and skin them carefully. Put them side by side in a saucepan and squeeze lemon juice over them. Add the syrup, the split vanilla pod and the champagne. Bring to the boil and simmer for about 20 minutes or until tender, turning the peaches over carefully from time to time.

Let them cool in their syrup and steep in it overnight or even for 2–3 days. Serve with the split vanilla pod laid across the top.

Peach Ice Cream with Crystallised Rose Petals

'One of the most important things for a housewife to remember is that hot things should be very hot and cold very cold or iced. Profit by the classic exclamation of a guest at Disraeli's table on arrival of the ice: "Ah, something really hot at last".'
Ruth Lowinsky LOVELY FOOD; A COOKERY NOTEBOOK 1931

Serves 6

2 lb (900 g) ripe peaches

8 oz (225 g) sugar

grated rind of 1 lemon

$\frac{1}{4}$ pint (150 ml) double cream

TO DECORATE

crystallised rose petals

Pour boiling water over the peaches and skin them. Put them in a saucepan into which they can be fitted side by side, with 1 pint (550 ml) water, the sugar and grated lemon rind. Bring to the boil and simmer for about 20 minutes or until completely tender, turning them from time to time. Allow to cool, then remove the stones from the peaches and put them with their syrup into a liquidiser or food processor and reduce to a purée. When it is completely cold, add the cream. Transfer the mixture to an ice cream maker or freezer tray and freeze. If you are using a tray in the freezer, beat the ice from time to time as it starts to harden; better still, whizz it in a food processor.

If you like, you can crack the peach stones with nutcrackers, skin the kernels and add them to the ice cream.

TO SERVE

Decorate with crystallised cream or peach coloured rose petals. To make them, paint the rose petals with egg white, lightly forked with a pinch of salt (but not beaten). Dip them in caster sugar and leave to dry for 2–3 hours on a rack.

The garden at the Old School House, Langford, Oxfordshire

Rose Petal Sorbet

The most fragrant roses of all are the deep red or crimson musk roses, but any rose with a heavy perfume will make a good sorbet. If you were lucky enough to have masses of Parma violets, you could also make a violet petal sorbet. This sorbet should be a very soft pink and have a tiny edge of bitterness from the Campari to cut the sweetness.

Serves 4

1 pint (550 ml) jug full of rose petals from very fragrant roses

7 oz (200 g) sugar

2 strips lemon rind

a few drops of rosewater

juice of ½ lemon

2 tbsp Campari

1 egg white

Put the rose petals in a big bowl. Dissolve the sugar in 1 pint (550 ml) water over a low heat, add the lemon rind and bring to the boil. Boil for 5 minutes, then pour the liquid over the rose petals. Leave to cool and infuse.

When the syrup is cold, strain it and add the lemon juice, rosewater and Campari.

Lightly beat the egg white and fold it into the syrup. Transfer the mixture to a sorbetière or freezer tray and freeze. If you are using a freezer tray, tip out the mixture when it is frozen to a slush and whizz it in a food processor or liquidiser, then freeze it again. You can decorate the sorbet with the crystallised rose petals described on page 121.

Blackcurrant Leaf Sorbet

A similar sorbet can be made with the leaves of rose-geraniums, that good-natured and heavily scented geranium with small, deeply crinkled leaves, or with fresh mint leaves, or with lemon verbena. I have also eaten a sweet thyme sorbet and a marjoram sorbet, very exciting if they are served together with scoops of mint sorbet arranged in a little herbal, tri-petalled flower.

Serves 4

1 lemon

10 oz (300 g) caster sugar

3–4 handfuls young blackcurrant leaves

dash of champagne (or white wine)

1 egg white

Pare the rind of the lemon in thin strips, and put into a pan with the sugar and 1 pint (550 ml) water. Dissolve the sugar over a low heat then turn up the heat, bring to the boil and boil for 5 minutes.

Put the currant leaves in a bowl and pour on the boiling syrup. Leave to cool; the flavour of the leaves will permeate the syrup. Strain it when cold.

Squeeze the juice from the lemon and add it with the champagne to the syrup. Now add the egg white. If you are using a sorbetière for freezing, add the egg white unbeaten; if you are using the freezer, beat the egg white to a soft foam first. Turn the mixture into the sorbetière, or into a freezer tray, and freeze. If you are using the freezer take out the mixture when it is slushy and whizz it in a food processor or liquidiser, then freeze it again. This will make all the difference to the texture and, funnily enough, to the colour, which becomes paler and more dazzling.

TO SERVE

Decorate each plate with a couple of small fresh blackcurrant leaves.

Pure Pineapple Sorbet

A good way of using an over-ripe pineapple.

Serves 4

1 large very ripe pineapple

1 tbsp Kirsch

1 tbsp caster sugar

1 egg white

lemon juice if necessary

Peel the pineapple with a sharp knife, quarter it, and remove the core. Cut it in pieces and reduce to a very fine purée in the liquidiser. Rub the purée through a sieve.

Add the Kirsch and sugar to taste and the egg white: if you are using a sorbetière for freezing, add the egg white unbeaten; if you are using the freezer, beat the egg white to a soft foam first. Taste the mixture and if necessary add a little lemon juice. Some pineapples have just the right balance of sweet with acid and others will need help, before they have enough flavour.

Freeze in a sorbetière or in a container in the freezer — if using the second method remove when frozen to a slush and whizz in the liquidiser or food processor, return to the container, refreeze and repeat when almost completely frozen.

TO SERVE

Remove from the freezer 25–30 minutes before you want to eat it.

BREAD, BISCUITS, CAKES AND PASTRY

People who like cooking seem to be divided into those who can make good pastry and those who can't. The latter are in plentiful supply, and there is no redeeming their leaden pastry no matter what lovely pie-fillings lie underneath or on top of it. The best pastry is the sort that arrives from the oven looking crisp or puffy and tastes as though it would blow away in a puff of air.

The thing to develop is a lightness of touch. Flour, once it is in contact with moisture, becomes tougher the more you handle it. This is because it contains gluten in little clumps which join up together and become harder and more elastic the more you work at it, either by beating, kneading or stirring the dough. This is exactly what you want if you are making bread dough and exactly what you don't want in pastry, cakes and scones. So the more briefly and lightly you handle or work the flour, the lighter the results will be.

For this reason, it is important when making cakes not to beat or whisk the mixture once the flour has gone in. Fold in the flour as quickly as possible and leave it at that; don't even do it too thoroughly. Scones are best mixed in seconds, and the less you actually touch your pastry with your fingers, the better.

So if, like many West Country housewives, you do a lot of baking and work very confidently and rapidly, you will get the best results.

Reed combers taking a break, North Devon

124

Old-Fashioned Potato Bread

'Thin bread and butter ... with a pot of homemade jam, which had been hidden away for such an occasion, and a dish of lettuce, fresh from the garden and garnished with little rosy radishes, made an attractive little meal, fit, as they said, to put before anybody.

In winter, salt butter would be sent for and toast would be made and eaten with celery. Toast was a favourite dish ... "I've made them a stack o' toast as high as up to their knees", a mother would say on a winter Sunday afternoon before her hungry brood came in from church. Another dish upon which they prided themselves was thin slices of cold boiled streaky bacon on toast, a dish so delicious that it deserves to be more widely popular.'

Flora Thompson LARK RISE TO CANDLEFORD 1939

This old-fashioned bread has a most delicious flavour and a moist, chewy texture such as bread ought to have. The colour is warm and creamy.

Threshing, North Devon

Makes 1 large free-form loaf or
2 × 1 lb (450 g) tin loaves

1 lb (450 g) mealy potatoes
1 lb (450 g) strong plain white bread flour
1½–2 tsp salt
½ oz (15 g) dried yeast
½ tsp sugar
¼ pint (150 ml) milk
½ oz (15 g) melted butter
extra flour for dusting

Cook the potatoes, drain and mash them, then purée them or put through a mouli-légumes to get out all the lumps; keep them warm. They should be dry and fluffy.

Put the flour in a warmed bowl, and mix the salt in with your hand. Mix the yeast with 4 tbsp warm water and the sugar, and leave in a warm place to froth up.

Mix the warm potatoes into the flour. Heat the milk and ¼ pint (150 ml) water to 105–115°F (40–46°C). Add the milk and water, the yeast mixture and melted butter to the potatoes and flour. Mix to a soft dough and then turn out on to a floured board. Knead it well for at least 5 minutes, sprinkling more flour on the board as it is needed. Then put back into the cleaned bowl, cover the top of the bowl with cling film and leave in a warm place to rise. This may take longer than your normal bread, but do not worry, it will come up eventually. When it is three times its original volume, punch it down and work for a few seconds, then shape into a big round loaf. Put it on a buttered baking sheet, prick the top here and there with a wooden fork and sprinkle well with flour. Cover with a cloth and leave in a warm place to prove for 40 minutes or until well risen and springy.

Meanwhile preheat the oven to 375°F (190°C, Gas 5). When the loaf is wobbly when you shake it, put it in the middle of the preheated oven and bake for 1 hour or more, until it is hollow when tapped. Cool on a wire rack.

Guy's bakery, Exbourne, North Devon

Brown Soda Bread

Traditional Irish country bread, made without yeast. The buttermilk is very important; as well as activating the raising agents it keeps the bread moist and gives it flavour.

12 oz (350 g) wholemeal flour

4 oz (100 g) plain white flour

1 tsp bicarbonate of soda

1 tsp cream of tartar

1½ tsp salt

1 oz (25 g) butter

½ pint (300 ml) buttermilk

Preheat the oven to 425°F (225°C, Gas 7).

Mix the flours, bicarbonate of soda, cream of tartar and salt together. Rub in the butter. Pour the buttermilk into the flour and knead well on a floured board for a few minutes.

Shape into a flattened round and cut a cross right across the middle. Sprinkle the top lightly with flour and place carefully on a greased baking sheet. Bake for 30–40 minutes, until golden and just cooked through — test with a skewer.

Remove to a rack, cover the loaf lightly with a slightly damp cloth and allow to cool.

TO SERVE

Eat sliced, with butter, preferably the same day as it is made.

One-rising Brown Bread

'Give me for a beautiful sight, a neat and smart woman, heating her oven and setting in her bread! And if the bustle does make the sign of labour glisten on her brow, where is the man who would not kiss that off, rather than lick the plaster from the cheek of a duchess? And what is the result? Why, good, wholesome food, sufficient for a considerable family for a week, prepared in three or four hours.'
William Cobbett COTTAGE ECONOMY 1830

Eat this good wholesome food as fresh as possible, or freeze it. It doesn't keep quite as well as two-rising brown loaves, but it is exceptionally quick to make and very good. Use fresh yeast; dried yeast seems to take longer and doesn't, in this case, give such good results.

Makes 3 × 1 lb (450 g) loaves

3 lb (1.3 kg) wholemeal stoneground flour

3 tsp salt (optional)

2 oz (50 g) butter

1½ oz (40 g) fresh yeast

1 tsp honey

1 tbsp molasses

Put 2½ lb (1.1 kg) flour and the salt into a large bowl, rub in the butter and leave in a warm place.

Mix the yeast into ½ pint (300 ml) lukewarm water, add the honey and leave in a warm place for 10 minutes or so to froth up. Don't let it get too hot — hand hot is right for fresh yeast — much hotter and it will be killed. Dissolve the molasses in 1 pint (550 ml) lukewarm water.

Make a well in the centre of the flour and pour in the liquids. Stir it all together and then start to knead the dough with your hands. When it forms a cohesive mass in the bowl, flour a work surface and tip out the dough.

Knead it for 5 minutes, slowly adding more flour as it is needed. You may end up with about 4 oz (100 g) flour left over. Divide the dough, which should be very light and springy, into three pieces. Form into loaves by making a flat oval and then rolling this up. Tuck the ends of each roll underneath and lower them into well-buttered tins. Cover with a cloth and leave to rise for 15 minutes in a warm place (not too hot), or until well risen and springy. Preheat the oven to 400°F (200°C, Gas 6). Bake the loaves for 40 minutes. Cool on a wire rack.

VARIATION

As a very good alternative use half wholemeal and half granary flour.

Bramble Scones

This is a lovely autumn recipe, particularly useful in the country when you have been out walking and picked a few handfuls of blackberries, but not enough to make jam or jelly.

Makes 6–8

4 oz (100 g) plain flour

2 tsp baking powder

½ oz (15 g) caster sugar

2 oz (50 g) butter, diced

2 oz (50 g) blackberries, very ripe

2 tbsp cream

milk and granulated sugar for glazing

Preheat the oven to 400°F (200°C, Gas 6). Sieve the flour, baking powder and sugar into a bowl, rub in the butter with your fingers until it looks like coarse crumbs, then drop in the blackberries.

Mix the cream in with your fingers, adding a little more if necessary to make a light, soft dough. Work lightly — the less it is handled the better. Roll the dough out lightly ½ inch (1 cm) thick and cut into 2½ inch (6 cm) circles. Brush with milk, sprinkle with coarse sugar, place on a buttered and floured baking sheet and bake for 10–15 minutes.

Eat the scones while they are still warm, buttered. You can use well-drained frozen blackberries instead of fresh — they are very good too. They look very countrified, not very even, and wonderfully home-made.

Scotch Pancakes *or* Drop Scones

These small soft pancakes are very quick to make. I have tried many different methods; the best are made with plain flour, bicarbonate of soda and cream of tartar, not with baking powder nor with self-raising flour. I like them plain, fresh and warm, served with butter and honey or jam. Serve them in a napkin.

Makes 16–20

7 oz (200 g) plain flour

½ tsp bicarbonate of soda

1 tsp cream of tartar

¼ tsp salt

pinch of sugar (optional)

2 eggs

½ pint (300 ml) milk or a little less

lard for frying

Sieve the flour, bicarbonate of soda, cream of tartar, salt and sugar into a bowl. Beat the eggs and stir them into the flour, gradually beating in the milk until you have a thickish, creamy batter.

Grease a griddle or a heavy iron frying pan lightly with lard and heat it until it is faintly smoking. Drop tablespoons of the mixture on to the hot plate, and when fairly large bubbles start to rise to the surface, flip the pancakes over carefully with a spatula. They should be well risen, nicely marked like tortoiseshell and a golden brown on both sides.

Brown Scones

'That afternoon, when Laura arrived, a little round table in the hearthplace had already been laid for tea. And what a meal! There were boiled new-laid eggs and scones and honey and home-made jam and, to crown all, a dish of fresh Banbury cakes. The carrier had a standing order to bring . . . a dozen of those cakes each market day.'
Flora Thompson LARK RISE TO CANDLEFORD 1939

Makes 8–10

8 oz (225 g) wheatmeal flour or 6 oz (175 g) wholemeal and 2 oz (50 g) plain white flour

2 tsp baking powder

pinch of salt

2 oz (50 g) butter

3 tbsp milk or buttermilk

3–4 tbsp cream

Preheat the oven to 375°F (190°C, Gas 5). Mix the flour or flours, baking powder and salt. Rub in the butter. Add enough milk or buttermilk and cream to make a light dough — handle it as little as possible.

Roll it out to ½ inch (1 cm) thick and cut into 2½ inch (6 cm) rounds. Or make smaller scones, no more than 2 inches (5 cm) across but ¾ inch (2 cm) thick, according to what sort of tea you are having. If it is a farmhouse or country tea have the large scones, if it's all small sandwiches and silver teapots have the smaller ones.

Bake on a buttered and floured baking sheet for 15 minutes.

TO SERVE

Eat while still warm, split and spread with plenty of butter. Home-made raspberry or strawberry jam and clotted or whipped cream make a proper 'Cream Tea' out of these scones.

Bringing in the hay, Deckport Farm, Hatherleigh, North Devon

Crumpets

"'I turns out with muffins and crumpets, sir, in October and continues until the spring, according to the weather" and whose "best customers is genteel houses 'cause I sells a genteel thing . . . we're a great convenience to the ladies, sir — a great convenience to them as likes a slap-up tea".'
A boy muffin-seller, quoted in Mayhew's *London Labour and the London Poor*
Cyril Ray THE GOURMET'S COMPANION 1963

As the muffin seller says, crumpets are a lovely thing to serve for tea in the dreaded dark afternoons of winter, best of all toasted in front of a fire, on a toasting fork. They take a bit of practice to get right.

Makes 8–10

¼ pint (150 ml) milk
½ oz (15 g) unsalted butter
1 tsp dried yeast or ½ oz (15 g) fresh yeast
1 tsp sugar
8 oz (225 g) strong plain white bread flour
¾ tsp salt
½ tsp baking powder

Heat the milk and butter in a small saucepan. When the liquid comes to the boil remove from the heat and add 4 tbsp water. Let the mixture cool to just over blood heat, 105°F (40°C) for fresh yeast or 115°F (46°C) for dried. Add the yeast and sugar and leave in a warm place to froth.

Put the flour and salt in a warmed bowl and beat in the yeasty liquid with a wooden spoon. When you have a smooth batter, cover the bowl and leave in a warm place to rise for about an hour, until at least twice the volume.

Dissolve the baking powder in 3 tbsp warm water and stir it into the mixture. Let it rise once more for about 20 minutes.

Grease three 3 inch (7.5 cm) crumpet rings with handles and arrange them on a greased griddle. Heat the griddle (a large, heavy iron frying pan would do) and spoon 2 tbsp of the mixture into each ring. Cook until bubbles rise and set on the top, then lift off the rings, turn the crumpets and cook for 2–3 minutes more, or until lightly browned. Always put the batter into heated rings or it will stick. Allow to cool on a rack. Crumpets freeze well.

TO SERVE
Toast on both sides and butter well; you can serve jam or honey with crumpets but many people like them just plain buttered, perhaps sprinkled with a little salt.

griddle

Welsh Cakes

These little, light cakes are cooked on a griddle or girdle. The large, round, iron plate was once hung by its hooped handle over the fire, but can be heated over a gas or electric ring. Modern designs have a handle more like a saucepan — or some cookers have a griddle built into the hob. Before griddles put in their appearance Welsh Cakes would have been cooked on a bakestone — a large heated stone or iron plate — or in more modest kitchens, on the hot hearthstone itself, swept clean of ash. If you do not have a griddle a stout iron frying pan will do.

Makes 10–12

8 oz (225 g) plain flour
pinch of salt
3 oz (75 g) sugar
½ tsp ground mace
¼ tsp bicarbonate of soda
¼ tsp cream of tartar
2 oz (50 g) butter
1–2 oz (25–50 g) lard
3 oz (75 g) sultanas or currants
1 egg, well beaten
a little milk

Sieve the flour, salt, sugar, mace, bicarbonate of soda and cream of tartar together into a bowl. Rub in the butter and lard until the mixture resembles breadcrumbs. Stir in the sultanas or currants and then add beaten egg and enough milk to make a stiffish dough.

Roll out the dough fairly thinly on a floured surface and cut out rounds with a 2 inch (5 cm) pastry cutter.

Heat the griddle or frying pan until it feels comfortably hot if you hold your hand about 1 inch (2.5 cm) above the surface. Rub the surface of the heated griddle with a piece of paper dipped into lard. Cook the cakes gently for 5–6 minutes on each side. Eat them warm, sprinkled with sugar or buttered.

Dundee Cake

'. . . all children and sensible people know that the fascination of tea really depends entirely on the cakes.'
Mrs C.F. Leyel and Miss Olga Hartley
THE GENTLE ART OF COOKERY 1925

The ground almonds make this a delicious cake, and one that keeps extremely well.

4 oz (100 g) currants

4 oz (100 g) sultanas

4 oz (100 g) raisins

4 oz (100 g) halved glacé cherries

5 oz (150 g) plain flour

4 oz (100 g) ground almonds

pinch of salt

6 oz (175 g) butter

6 oz (175 g) muscovado or other soft dark brown sugar

3 large eggs

1 tbsp whisky

12 whole blanched almonds for decorating the top

Preheat the oven to 325°F (160°C, Gas 3). Toss the currants, sultanas, raisins and cherries in 1 oz (25 g) of the flour. Mix the remaining flour, ground almonds and salt in a large bowl. Cream together the butter and sugar and beat the eggs. Add the flour mixture and eggs alternately to the butter and sugar mixture, working them in lightly with a wooden spoon. Gently blend in the whisky. Fold in the fruit carefully.

Line a deep 6 inch (16.5 cm) cake tin with buttered greaseproof paper and flour it. Turn the mixture into the tin and decorate the top with a ring of almonds. Bake for 1¾–2 hours, covering lightly with foil when the top looks cooked and the almonds light brown. Test with a skewer to see if the cake is done. Allow to cool in the tin and keep overnight before cutting.

Yorkshire Coffee Buns

Eat these fresh. Mrs Millson, a Yorkshire lady, who gave me this recipe, says they should be eaten as they are, not split and buttered. They are to eat with coffee, they do not have coffee in the ingredients.

Makes 10–12

8 oz (225 g) plain flour

2½ tsp baking powder

4 oz (100 g) Demerara sugar

2 oz (50 g) best plump sultanas

4 oz (100 g) butter at room temperature

1½ large or 2 small eggs

Preheat the oven to 350°F (180°C, Gas 4). Sieve the flour and baking powder and mix well in a bowl with the sugar and sultanas. Add the butter and well-beaten eggs and work everything together lightly with your hands to a soft paste.

Roll the paste out gently on a floured board to about ½ inch (1 cm) thick and cut into 2½ inch (4 cm) rounds with a plain cutter or a wine glass. Place on a baking sheet and bake in the top of the oven for 10 minutes — do not overbrown, they should be tan-coloured. Eat the buns as soon as they are cool; they are wonderfully light, crisp outside and soft inside.

Teacakes

These can be served for tea or breakfast, but should always be warm. If you like toasted teacakes, toast the cut sides only.

Makes 10–12

1 oz (25 g) fresh yeast (½ oz/15 g dried yeast)

¼ tsp sugar

2 lb (900 g) plain flour

1 tbsp salt

2 oz (50 g) butter

a few currants or sultanas (optional)

1 egg, beaten

¼ pint (150 ml) warm milk

Mix the yeast well with a few tablespoons of warm water and the sugar. Leave in a warm place to froth.

Put the flour and salt in a large bowl and rub in the butter with your fingertips. Add the currants or sultanas at this point if you want to include them. When the yeast is well frothed up, pour it into a well in the centre of the flour, add the beaten egg, warm milk and as much warm water as is needed to make a good, soft, pliable dough — about ½ pint (300 ml).

Put the mass of dough on a floured worktop, cover it with a cloth and let it rest whilst you wash out the bowl. This allows the flour to absorb the liquid thoroughly, making the dough easier to handle.

Now knead the dough thoroughly for 5–10 minutes until it is silky smooth. Put it back into the bowl, cover the top of the bowl with cling-film and put a folded tea towel on top to hold in the warmth. Leave it to rise in a warm kitchen for 2–3 hours or until it is more than double in size.

Punch down the dough, then take 4 oz (100 g) lumps at a time and shape them into round, flat cakes about 4 or 5 inches (10 or 12.5 cm) across. Dust lightly with flour. Cover loosely with a tea towel and leave to prove on greased baking sheets. Preheat the oven to 350–375°F (180–190°C, Gas 4–5). When the teacakes have become soft and slightly puffy, bake them for 30–35 minutes.

Split in half while still warm, butter and then cut in quarters.

Whist Drive refreshments, Beaford, North Devon

The church garden party, Chulmleigh Rectory, North Devon

Janetta's Well-known Chocolate Cake

'There was an old person of Rheims
Who was troubled by terrible dreams;
So, to keep him awake, they fed him with cake,
Which amused that old person of Rheims.'
from THE COMPLETE NONSENSE OF EDWARD LEAR

Janetta Jackson invented this cake to serve in her restaurant La Fonda in Marbella. It has since become the favourite dessert in most of the restaurants up and down the Costa del Sol.

Make it in a 12½ inch (32 cm) flat flan tin with a removable base. The idea is that it is a wide shallow cake, rather than a small deep one. It's much easier to serve and eat as it doesn't tip over on the plate and every slice has a very generous amount of icing. The cake itself is meant to be fudgey and not, like so many horrible modern cakes, all airy and fluffy and dry. If you haven't got a large enough tin, use a small roasting tin lined with foil.

Serves 10–12

8½ oz (240 g) dark chocolate — the darker the better, bitter Suchard is good

8½ oz (240 g) caster sugar

6½ oz (180 g) softened butter

6 eggs, separated

6 tbsp self-raising flour

ICING

6½ oz (180 g) dark chocolate

10 sugar lumps dissolved in a little black coffee

2 oz (50 g) butter

Butter the tin and preheat the oven to 400°F (200°C, Gas 6). Melt the chocolate in the oven. Beat the sugar, butter and egg yolks to a cream, and stir in the chocolate.

Sift the flour and fold it in and lastly whisk the egg whites to a firm snow and fold them in. Transfer the mixture to the flan tin, bake for 30–35 minutes, remove the outer ring of the tin and leave it to cool.

FOR THE ICING

Melt the chocolate in the top of a double boiler with the sugar and coffee. Cut the butter into pieces and stir the chocolate into it, beating until smooth.

Spread the icing over the cake with a palette knife while it is still warm.

Janetta's Cherry Cake

Like the chocolate cake, this is a wide shallow cake, easy to cut into small slices to tempt people who normally wouldn't eat a piece of cake, or into large slices for people who love it.

1 lb (450 g) glacé cherries

9 oz (250 g) soft margarine

10 oz (300 g) caster sugar

grated rind of 1 large lemon

5 eggs, separated

5 oz (150 g) self-raising flour plus a little extra

icing sugar to decorate

Butter a 12½ inch (32 cm) flat flan tin and preheat the oven to 350°F (180°C, Gas 4). Put the cherries in a sieve and steam them over a pan of boiling water to remove excess syrup (I do this to prevent them sinking, it nearly always works). Then dry them in a cloth and toss them in a little flour.

Cream the margarine and sugar together in a bowl. Add the grated rind of the lemon. Whisk the egg yolks and stir them into the egg and sugar mixture. Sift in the flour and fold it in, then fold in the cherries.

Whisk the egg whites until they form stiff peaks and fold them into the mixture. Fill the tin and bake for 35–40 minutes. Allow to cool and dust with icing sugar. It should not be completely cooked, it is nicer slightly gooey, and keeps very well.

Musselburgh Gingerbread Cake

I based this cake on an original recipe in Dorothy Allhusen's lovely *Book of Scents and Dishes* written in 1926, in which she gives the names of all the friends whose recipes she publishes. In this case the originator was the Lord Elphinstone of Carberry Tower, Musselburgh. He must have been a keen gourmet. Incidentally Musselburgh is the home of Scotland's only race course, and this would be a very good cake to take on a racing picnic.

12 oz (350 g) plain flour

1 oz (25 g) ground ginger

pinch of mixed ground spice

pinch of salt

8 oz (225 g) soft margarine

4 oz (100 g) black treacle

4 oz (100 g) golden syrup

4 eggs

4 oz (100 g) muscovado sugar

2 oz (50 g) whole candied orange peel, chopped

Preheat the oven to 350°F (180°C, Gas 4). Sift the flour, ginger and mixed spice in a bowl, with a pinch of salt. Work the margarine, treacle and syrup together in a bowl until they are smoothly blended. Beat the eggs and sugar together well and then add the treacle mixture and the chopped orange peel. Fold in the spiced flour.

Butter and flour a shallow 9 inch (23 cm) cake tin or an 8 inch (20 cm) square tin and put in the mixture. Bake for 1 hour, covering lightly with foil after half an hour to prevent the top from darkening or becoming tough. Allow to cool and settle overnight, before cutting. Keep wrapped in foil to prevent it from drying out.

Cheese and Oatmeal Biscuits

Makes about 20

8 oz (225 g) porridge oats or coarse oatmeal

4 oz (100 g) plain flour

2 oz (50 g) grated cheese — Cheddar, Cheshire, or Parmesan are all suitable

4 oz (100 g) butter

salt

cayenne pepper

1 egg

Preheat the oven to 325°F (160°C, Gas 3).

These biscuits can be made in a food processor. Process the porridge oats for a few seconds to make them finer but with a few larger pieces. Add the flour, cheese, butter, salt and cayenne and process quickly to a fine, crumbly, dryish mixture. Add the well-beaten egg and 3–4 tbsp water to bind the mixture lightly — keep it on the dryish side. If you are making the biscuits by hand, rub the butter into the flour and oatmeal, add the cheese, salt and cayenne and then stir in the well-beaten egg and enough water to bind the mixture as before.

Roll out the dough on a floured board. The dough will be quite crumbly round the edges, but this doesn't matter. Cut into rounds with a 2½ inch pastry cutter or wine glass and space the biscuits out on a buttered baking sheet. Bake for 20–25 minutes or a little longer — they should be cooked and crisp all the way through when they are cool, but not browned.

TO SERVE

Eat when cool with butter and cream cheese. Celery is rather good with these; use only the tender, pale yellow, inner stalks, and keep the stringy outer stalks for soups.

A kitchen dresser, Standlake, Oxfordshire

Brandy Snaps

Makes 25

4 tbsp golden syrup

4 oz (100 g) butter

4 oz (100 g) plain flour

4 oz (100 g) sugar

1 tsp ground ginger

1 tsp brandy

Preheat the oven to 350°F (180°C, Gas 4).

Heat the syrup in a small saucepan. When it comes to the boil, add the butter and let it melt completely, shaking the pan. Remove the pan from the heat and stir in the remaining ingredients to obtain a thick smooth batter.

Drop teaspoons of the mixture, well-spaced to allow for spreading, on an ungreased baking sheet. Bake for 6–7 minutes to an even golden colour.

Remove the sheet from the oven and allow to cool for about 1 minute. Then remove the brandy snaps one at a time with a palette knife, and roll them into cylinders round the handle of a wooden spoon. Work fast because the brandy snaps set quickly and become brittle.

TO SERVE

The little cylinders, when cool and crisp, can be filled with whipped cream, flavoured, if you like, with brandy; or they can be eaten as they are.

Rough Puff Pastry

'Dear Nelly!
Learn with care the pastry art,
And mind the easy precepts I impart;
Draw out your dough elaborately thin,
And cease not to fatigue your rolling pin:
Of eggs and butter see you mix enough,
For then the paste will swell into a puff,
Which will in crumpling sounds your praise report
And eat, as housewives speak, exceeding short.'
Quoted by D. Hartley FOOD IN ENGLAND 1954 and
attributed to William King (1663–1712)

8 oz (225 g) butter straight from the refrigerator

8 oz (225 g) plain flour

a little salt

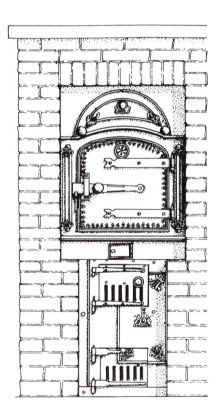

Cut the butter into little cubes.

Sieve the flour and salt into a bowl, add the butter and cut it into the flour with a sharp knife until it is in pea-size pieces. Add 1 tbsp cold water and stir it in with the knife blade then add 1–2 tbsp more until you can gather the dough into a ball. Flatten the ball, score it twice with a knife and wrap in foil. Chill for 20 minutes.

Roll the dough out into a rectangle 12 by 6 inches (30 by 15 cm) and fold into three like a purse. Turn it round 90° and roll and fold again. Use flour to prevent the pastry from sticking but not too much at a time, as it will make the pastry heavy. Chill for 15 minutes.

Repeat the rolling and folding 2 or 3 times more, chilling in between each folding operation. Use whenever a recipe calls for puff or flaky pastry, and for pies.

CRIMPING THE EDGE OF A PIE

There are several ways of making the edge of a pie crust look pretty and stick firmly to its pie dish.

1. The first is the simple fork method — use the prongs of a form to make a ridged pattern all the way round the edge. Keep the fork at an angle towards the centre of the pie so that the cut edge of the pastry does not become flattened.
2. Scallop the edge by pressing the rim with your thumb or the handle end of a spoon, while making a vertical dent in the cut edge of the pastry with the back of knife at the side of every thumbprint.
3. Using a small, old-fashioned meat skewer with a round loop top, press the top into the rim of the pastry all the way round; keep it at an angle to avoid flattening the cut edge of the pastry. This gives a pretty pattern of circles, each circle just touching the next one.
4. If you have a deep rim, such as the rim of a plate pie, make diagonal lines in the edge, close together, with the back of a knife blade, so that the pie looks as though it is spinning.
5. For a pasty or free-form pie, frill the edge. Press the two layers of pastry together and give it a wavy edge by pinching with the fore-fingers and thumbs of both hands at once.

Shortcrust Flan Case

*'The greatest possible cleanliness and nicety should
be observed in making pastry. The slab or board,
paste-rollers, tins, cutters, moulds, everything, in
fact, used for it, and especially the hands, should be
equally free from the slightest soil or particle of
dust. The more expeditiously the finer kinds of paste
are made and dispatched to the oven, and the less
they are touched, the better.'*
Eliza Acton MODERN COOKERY FOR PRIVATE
FAMILIES 1845

For open pies, tarts and so forth. Salty, crisp English
butter gives the right texture and flavour to the
pastry.

Makes one 9½ inch (24 cm) flan case

5 oz (150 g) plain flour

1 oz (25 g) self-raising flour

4 oz (100 g) very cold butter

TO MAKE SHORTCRUST PASTRY

Sieve the two flours together into a bowl. Cut the
butter into the flour with a knife, holding the butter
in one hand and carving off thin flakes of butter with
the other. Rub the flakes quickly into the flour —
stop as soon as the mixture starts to become heavy
and clings to your fingers. The butter should not be
too fine — the texture of coarse large crumbs is
about right.

Add water — a couple of tablespoons at first and
then a little at a time until you can just collect the
pastry together into a mass. Form it into a ball,
cover and chill for an hour in the refrigerator.

To use it, beat it briefly with a rolling pin to
loosen it and roll it out on a floured board.

TO MAKE THE FLAN CASE

Line a well-buttered flan tin with the pastry, prick
the base with a fork and trim the edges, pushing the
pastry neatly into the sides of the tin. Fill with
crumpled foil and chill, or bake at once.

Allow 12–15 minutes at 375°F (190°C, Gas 5) and
then remove the foil and add the filling. If it is to be
served cold and will not get any more cooking in the
oven, turn down the heat to 325°F (160°C, Gas 3)
and allow a further 10–15 minutes without the foil.

Norah Maynard serving tea, Atherington, Devon

Iddesleigh, North Devon, in the drought

SAUCES, PICKLES AND PRESERVES

We make sauces as a sort of ritual, and each sauce has its own particular purpose. Apple sauce with roast pork, bread sauce with game, mint sauce with lamb, parsley sauce or Cumberland sauce with ham, horseradish sauce with beef: all are either soothing or refreshing and the perfect antidote to rich meats. To these typical sauces of the English table add the occasional hollandaise and mayonnaise for summer dishes and for fish, and the beloved white or bécha-mel sauce made with parsley or watercress or prawns, and you have the best of them. Make no mistake, they have an integrity and rightness about them and are just the very thing that sets British cooking apart from the suave, rich-sauced cuisine of our neighbours.

The quality of any meal shows in the details, and if you take the trouble to make your own jam, mar-malade and preserves, you can be certain that, due to our collective ancestral instincts for preserving and squirrelling things away for lean times, you will not only have much finer jams and jellies and better chutneys than money can possibly buy, you will also gain the most disproportionate sense of satisfaction.

Although it is traditional to make chutney out of marrow and green tomatoes, I find both these are watery and tasteless; much nicer, better-flavoured chutneys can be made with ripe tomatoes, peppers, apples and oranges, ingredients that have a good flavour of their own.

Bread Sauce

*'All milk puddings, baked suet puddings, which are
even better than boiled ones, mince pies,
doughnuts, and brandy snaps, also Scotch Woodcock
and cheese straws, are all well within the powers of
the plainest English Cook, and come as a surprise,
or even a shock, as in the case of bread sauce, to
foreigners.'*
Ruth Lowinsky LOVELY FOOD; A COOKERY
NOTEBOOK 1931

Bread sauce is a lovely old-fashioned thing to serve with roast chicken, roast game (particularly pheasant) or with turkey. French people are utterly appalled when they first catch sight of it, but find they rather like it and even ask for more.

Serves 6

2 oz (50 g) fresh white breadcrumbs

¾ pint (425 ml) milk

1 shallot

1 bayleaf

5 black peppercorns

pinch of cayenne pepper

pinch of ground mace

pinch of ground nutmeg

4 cloves

salt and freshly ground white pepper

2½ fl oz (60 ml) double cream

Heat the milk with the peeled shallot, bayleaf, peppercorns, spices and a little salt. Let it simmer gently for 15–20 minutes without boiling.

Strain the milk and add the breadcrumbs. Leave off the heat to soak. This part of the preparation can be done well in advance.

TO SERVE
Heat the sauce through and beat with a wooden spoon. Season with salt if needed and white pepper and add the cream. Serve hot.

Cumberland Sauce

Makes ½ pint (300 ml)

2 shallots

1 orange

1 lemon

1 piece fresh ginger, 1 inch (2.5 cm) square

1 small glass port

8 oz (225 g) redcurrant jelly

salt and cayenne pepper

Peel and chop the shallots and cook in a small quantity of boiling water for 2 minutes. Drain.

Pare the rind of the orange and lemon thinly and cut it into fine julienne (matchstick) strips. Drop them into a pan of boiling water and blanch for a couple of minutes, then drain. Cut the peeled ginger into fine julienne strips.

Squeeze the juice from the orange and lemon and put it in a pan with the port, redcurrant jelly, shallots, julienne of orange, lemon and ginger, and a little salt and cayenne.

Cook until smooth and syrupy and serve hot or cold with glazed ham, roast venison or cold meat.

Mint Sauce

Serves 4

3 large handfuls of fresh mint leaves

2–3 tsp granulated sugar

4 tbsp wine vinegar

Wash and shake the mint leaves, sprinkle them with sugar and chop rather finely. Put in a bowl. Heat the vinegar and pour it over the mint. Add more sugar if you think the sauce is too sharp. Serve hot or cold.

ALTERNATIVE
Use lemon juice instead of vinegar and you can also add a little olive oil. This is not traditional mint sauce, being much less violent in flavour, but it is exceptionally good.

Baked Apple Sauce

This sauce is extremely easily made if you are roasting a duck, goose or piece of pork. By baking the apples you obtain a more concentrated flavour.

Serves 4–6

2 huge Bramleys

4 tsp sugar

pinch of salt

2 nuts of butter

Simply score the skin of the apples all the way round their circumference, and put them into the oven in a dish on the rack alongside or underneath the roasting tin. Let them bake until they are soft right through: test with a skewer and remove them when ready (they will be all puffy with blackened skin). Scrape out the cooked soft apple, almost a purée already. Discard the core. Mix the pulp quickly with sugar, salt and butter and keep hot. The baking gives the apples a particularly good, mellow flavour.

Parsley Sauce

Eat parsley sauce with all kinds of poached fish, including smoked haddock, and with boiled bacon or gammon. It is a very good sauce, and not to be despised or forgotten.

Makes 1 pint (550 ml), enough for 6 people

1 pint (550 ml) creamy milk

1 bayleaf

1 onion

12 black peppercorns

1 oz (25 g) butter

1 oz (25 g) flour

salt and pepper

1 bunch of parsley

cream (optional)

Heat the milk gently with the bayleaf, peeled, sliced onion and peppercorns, and let it infuse on the side of the stove for at least 10 minutes to absorb the flavours.

Melt the butter in a pan, stir in the flour, let it bubble for a minute, then remove from the heat and cool a little. Strain in the hot milk, whisking all the time. Season, return to the heat and stir over medium heat for 5 minutes.

Chop the parsley and add it to the sauce. Stir it in for a few minutes, but no longer or it will lose its colour. You can add a dash of cream now if you like.

Watercress Sauce

This sauce is an interesting alternative to Parsley Sauce, and is rather less day-to-day. Eat with any member of the salmon family, with turbot, brill or halibut, or with boiled gammon or chicken croquettes (page 79).

Serves 4–6

1½ bunches of watercress

1 large onion

1 stick of celery

¾ pint (425 ml) milk

1 bayleaf

¾ oz (20 g) butter

¾ oz (20 g) flour

dash of white wine vinegar

3 tbsp double cream

salt and white mignonette pepper

Wash the watercress thoroughly, trim off the roots and any damaged leaves and chop it. Set aside.

Chop the peeled onion and the celery. Heat the milk with the chopped onion and celery and the bayleaf. Let it infuse for 5 minutes.

Melt the butter in a pan, stir in the flour and let it cook gently for 3–4 minutes without browning. Allow it to cool a little then strain in the milk, away from the heat. Return to the heat and whisk until it thickens; add the wine vinegar, cream and seasoning. Cook for a few minutes and taste it — the basic sauce should taste good in its own right. When you have achieved this, add the cleaned, chopped watercress. Stir it in and cook gently for 2 minutes to bring out the flavour.

MIGNONETTE PEPPER
This is a coarse pepper, pounded in a mortar with a pestle rather than ground in a grinder. Use white peppercorns when you don't want to spoil the colour of your sauce.

Lady Sysonby's Cream Horseradish Sauce

Lady Sysonby says, 'This is a ... good sauce for chicken or game, and also excellent with either hot or cold salmon.' I think she is right about the salmon and I found it absolutely excellent with smoked trout — roast beef on the other hand seems to demand the traditional version (see page 54).

Serves 6

½ tsp mustard

½ tsp sugar

½ tsp tarragon vinegar

2 tbsp grated horseradish

2½ fl oz (65 ml) double cream, slightly whipped

pinch of salt — my addition

Mix the ingredients in the order given, stirring in the cream very lightly. Stand on ice.

'TARAGON VINEGAR
To a quart of the best white wine vinegar take a small handful of Taragon, stalks and altogether, twist the stalks well with your hands that the vinegar may get out all the strength of the Taragon the quicker, put the Taragon in an earthen jug or pan, and pour the vinegar upon it, let it stand to infuse 24 hours, then you may try if it's strong enough for your tast, if not, stir it up and let it stand longer, or add more Taragon as you think proper, then strain from the Taragon thro' a fine linnen cloth and bottle it; it will keep as long as you please.'
THE RECEIPT BOOK OF ELIZABETH RAPER
1756–70

In the kitchen at Great Dixter, East Sussex

Horseradish and Walnut Sauce

'I know plenty of men who would break up their homes (after serving the furniture in the same way) and emigrate; who would go on strike, were roast beef to be served at the dinner-table unaccompanied by horse-radish sauce.'
Edward Spencer CAKES AND ALE 1897

Makes ½ pint (300 ml)

½ pint (300 ml) double cream

1 oz (25 g) grated horseradish, fresh or bottled

½ tsp mild Dijon mustard

pinch of sugar

1 tbsp wine vinegar or tarragon vinegar

2 tbsp chopped walnuts, preferably fresh

salt

Lightly whip the cream until it thickens but is still smooth. Stir in the remaining ingredients and allow to stand for 20 minutes. Serve with roast beef, hot or cold, or with cold fish such as cod or bass.

Garam Masala

British cooks have a long tradition of making their own version of Indian curry, a favourite since the days of the Raj. You will not find curry powder on the shelf in most Indian kitchens, but you will find garam masala. Used on its own or in addition to curry powder, it gives an aromatic lift to many plain and simple dishes. Unlike curry powder, it is sprinkled over the top of the food towards the end of the cooking.

Makes about 5 tbsp

2 tbsp cumin seeds

1 tbsp black peppercorns

16 cloves, bruised with a hammer

4 cardamom seeds, bruised with a hammer

Use a clean coffee grinder to grind the spices to a powder. Sieve and store in an airtight jar.

Best Salad Dressing

'The oil must be very clean, not highly coloured or yellow, but with an eye, rather, of pallid olive green.'
John Evelyn ACETARIA, A DISCOURSE OF SALLETS 1699

Salad dressings can be varied according to the type of salad used. A delicate flavoured lettuce heart salad could be made with shallots instead of garlic, lemon juice and perhaps some chopped tarragon or chives in it, while a tougher salad such as curly endive needs a good strong dressing with plenty of garlic, wine vinegar and really strong olive oil — if you are not a garlic lover, try rubbing two little pieces of fried bread with a clove of garlic and put them in the bowl underneath the salad.

½–1 clove garlic, depending on the size

salt and plenty of coarse black pepper

1 tsp mild Dijon mustard

2 tsp white wine vinegar or lemon juice

5 tbsp virgin olive oil

small pinch of sugar if liked

This can be done very fast if you have all the ingredients on hand in one corner of the kitchen. Chop the clove of garlic and then crush it to a fine paste with some salt sprinkled on it — the salt gives friction and absorbs the juices from the garlic; use a stainless steel knife. Put it in a small bowl, mix in the mustard, add the vinegar or lemon juice and then add the oil, gradually whisking it in with a fork or a small whisk so that you have a thick emulsion. (If it separates it doesn't really matter, but the emulsified version coats the salad beautifully and doesn't all collect in the bottom of the salad bowl.)

The quantities of garlic or vinegar vary with their strength — some garlic is very mild, some very pungent, vinegar can be vicious or mellow, so always taste the dressing and adjust it if necessary. I have made quite a small quantity, when using larger quantities don't double up on the garlic or it becomes overpowering.

Planting lettuces, Eggesford, North Devon

Rich Salad Dressing

Avocados are not strictly British I'm afraid, but then neither are lemons, a well established ingredient of salad dressing, nor a host of other things we have happily integrated into our cooking. However, this dressing was invented by an English friend and on a salad of mixed green leaves — different sorts of lettuce, young spinach leaves, lamb's lettuce, chicory, red chicory, watercress, endive, rocket if you can get it, flat parsley and chervil for example — it makes all the difference.

1 small mild onion
1 small avocado
2–3 tsp lemon juice
5 tbsp olive oil
salt and a pinch of sugar

Peel and chop the onion and avocado coarsely and mix in the salad bowl with the other ingredients. Leave in the bottom of the salad bowl and put the salad servers side by side, ends crossed, in the bowl, so that they slightly cover the dressing—this stops the vegetables from going soggy. Put whatever you choose for the salad, well washed and dried in a cloth, on top. Mix all together well just before serving.

147

Red Tomato Chutney

This is the most delicious chutney in the world, wonderful with cold ham, pheasant or turkey, with pork pie and with all kinds of curry. In fact the recipe comes from a friend of mine whose mother lives in Delhi where the tomatoes are really rich and well flavoured. Ours tend to be more watery, so the chutney can take a long time to cook, but it gets there in the end.

Makes about 6 lb (2.6 kg)

4½ lb (2 kg) tomatoes, firm and red

1 whole head of garlic

1½ inch (4 cm) piece of whole fresh ginger

8 oz (225 g) sugar

1 tsp red chilli powder

2 tsp salt

2 tbsp olive oil

4 green chillies

4 oz (100 g) sultanas

½ tsp each cumin seeds, brown mustard seeds, fennel seeds and, if available, black onion seeds and fenugreek

¼ pint (150 ml) vinegar

Put the tomatoes in a bowl and pour boiling water over them to loosen the skins, then remove the skins and cut the tomatoes into quarters. Put them in a large heavy saucepan. Peel all the cloves from the whole head of garlic, peel and slice the ginger and add them to the tomatoes with the sugar. Add the chilli powder and salt and cook gently until all the liquid has evaporated. Heat the oil — you can use mustard oil if you prefer — in a frying pan. Cook the chillies, sultanas and spices for a few seconds, then add them with their oil to the tomatoes and mix in well.

Add the vinegar and cook until it is almost evaporated and the chutney has a good, thick consistency. Put in hot jars and cover tightly. Allow to mature for two months before eating.

Orange Chutney

This is a particularly delicious chutney, dark, rich and hot. It comes from Claire Clifton and Martina Nicolls' *Edible Gifts*. We eat it with curry and with cold poultry and game, particularly turkey or chicken — I also sometimes use it in the sauce when making chicken curry.

Makes about 4–5 lb (1.8–2.2 kg)

4 large oranges

2 large cooking apples

4 oz (100 g) stem ginger (in syrup)

1 fresh chilli

2 tbsp currants or sultanas

juice of 1 extra orange

1 oz (25 g) salt

freshly ground black pepper

12 oz (350 g) soft brown sugar (or less)

3 tbsp honey

white wine or cider vinegar to cover

Peel the oranges, remove the pith and pips, slice the flesh and finely chop the peel. Peel, core and chop the apples. Drain and chop the ginger. Remove the stem and seeds from the chilli and chop it. Put the oranges, apples, ginger, chilli, currants, orange juice, salt and pepper into a saucepan. Cover and simmer until the oranges are tender. Add a bit more orange juice if it seems to be drying out.

Add the sugar to taste, honey and enough white wine or vinegar to cover the fruit. Mix well and boil *gently*, stirring occasionally, until it thickens. It will take about an hour.

Put into clean warm jars and cap with plastic-lined lids. Keep for at least a month to allow the chutney to mature before you eat it.

Pickled Red Cabbage

This used to be served with a good brown beef stew, but would also be excellent with cold beef or game, sausages or pork pies, or with bread and cheese.

Makes 2 lb (900 g)

1 medium red cabbage (1½–2 lb/675–900 g)

2 oz (50 g) salt

½ pint (300 ml) red wine vinegar

½ pint (300 ml) malt vinegar

2 dried whole chillies

4 cloves

1 tsp coriander seeds

2 tsp whole black peppercorns

1 piece fresh ginger, bruised

1 tsp juniper berries

2 blades of mace

4 tsp caster sugar

Remove the outside leaves of the cabbage, quarter it and cut out the core, then slice it and cut the slices into shorter lengths, to make it easier to eat. Put it in a bowl in layers, sprinkling each layer with salt; I use coarse Maldon sea salt, but any iodine-free salt will do. Weight the top with a plate, and leave for 24 hours, turning the cabbage from time to time.

Rinse well and drain. Put the vinegar into a pan with the spices and sugar, bring it to the boil and stand back or the fumes will almost make you faint. Simmer for 5 minutes and then leave to get cold. Pack the well-drained cabbage into clean preserving jars, strain the cold vinegar over the top and seal. Keep for 3 days and it will be ready.

'TO PICKLE GHIRKINS
Take Girkins and young cucumbers, put them in a jar, then take vinegar (enough to cover them) black pepper, a little alspice, some ginger, cloves, and some salt, bruise your spice and put it in a linnen bag, boil it in your vinegar and pour boiling hot on your girkins, and so do every day for a fortnight, keep the jar close covered.'
THE RECEIPT BOOK OF ELIZABETH RAPER
1756–70

Home-made produce on the Women's Institute market stall, Barnstaple, North Devon

Pickled Onions

'The love of pickles is sometimes considered the sign of a depraved taste: certainly it is a very widespread depravity. The desire for something at once hot, sour, salt and pungent would seem to be an inherent principle of human nature.'
May Byron POT LUCK 1914

This is the classic depraved pickled onion, absolutely essential with a ploughman's lunch of bread and cheese. It may blow the top of your head off the first time you try it, but it is addictive.

Makes 2 lb (900 g)

2 lb (900 g) pickling onions

8 oz (225 g) sea salt

FOR THE PICKLING VINEGAR

½ pint (300 ml) white malt vinegar

½ pint (300 ml) malt vinegar

2 dried whole chillies

4 cloves

1 tsp coriander seeds

2 tsp whole black peppercorns

1 blade of mace

1 piece of dried root ginger, bruised with a hammer

Pour boiling water over the onions, let them float in it for a minute then remove them, immerse briefly in cold water and peel. Alternatively peel them in a basin or bowl of cold water — these are both good ways of preventing yourself crying too much, and the first makes them easier to peel, but possibly a little less crisp.

Put them into a bowl and cover with 2 pints (1.1 litres) water in which you have dissolved the sea salt. Leave for 24 hours, drain and rinse.

Put the vinegar into a pan. Rinse the spices in a sieve and add them to the vinegar. Bring to the boil, boil for 5 minutes and allow to get cold. Strain the vinegar, reserving the chillies. Fill the jars with the onions, packing them in carefully and putting a red chilli in each jar, against the glass to look pretty. Fill to the top with spiced vinegar and cover with plastic-lined lids. Keep for at least a week before eating, a month would be even better. They will keep for several months.

Cranberry Jelly

Cranberries were at one time well known on the moors of Northern England and Scotland and the lovely, tart fruit was made into pies or served with game. This jelly is excellent with hot or cold turkey, venison or pheasant.

Makes about 2 lb (900 g)

5 sharp apples

12 oz (350 g) cranberries

juice and pips of 1 orange

juice and pips of 1 lemon

about 12 oz–1 lb (350–450 g) sugar

Peel and cut up the apples. Put all the ingredients, except the sugar, into a saucepan. Add 1 pint (550 ml) water and cook gently for an hour, stirring but not mashing. Strain the pulp through a jelly bag.

Measure the juice and add 1 lb (450 g) sugar to 1 pint (550ml) juice. Dissolve the sugar, stirring over a low heat. Then bring to the boil and boil rapidly until setting point is reached, about 10 minutes. To test whether it will set, spoon a little jelly on to a cold saucer; it should start to set as it cools. Or lift some on the wooden spoon and drop it slowly back into the pan; when it flakes off the spoon instead of running, it is ready to set.

Quickly skim any scum off the top and pour the jelly into small clean jars. Cover with discs of waxed paper and jam pot covers.

Jelly bag from
Good Plain Cookery, 1882

Redcurrant Jelly or Blackcurrant Jelly

Pick the currants on a dry, sunny day. Some people leave the stalks on, but I prefer to remove them for a finer tasting jelly. Do this with a fork, drawing it down each bunch, and the berries will come off very neatly.

Make the jelly by extracting the juice in a bain-marie, in exactly the same way as for bramble jelly (right). When you have strained the juice through a jelly bag, without squeezing it at all, measure it and allow 12 oz (350 g) sugar to every 1 pint (550 ml) juice. Put the juice into the preserving pan and boil for 5 minutes before adding the warmed sugar. Stir until it has all dissolved, then boil for a short time until setting point is reached. Redcurrants set very well and usually reach setting point in a few minutes.

'HOW TO TURN STRAWBERRY JAM WHITE Here's something for the children to make for their own tea; but they must make it for themselves, for the joy of seeing a red jam turn white. First, whisk together two egg-whites until the white will stand up on the whisk, then mix these with four ounces of strawberry jam and four ounces of redcurrant jelly, and go on whisking until, unbelievably, the mixture becomes white.'
Ambrose Heath GOOD FOOD FOR CHILDREN 1941

Violet Currant Jelly

Make this in exactly the same way as redcurrant jelly, but add 8 oz (225 g) blackcurrants to 2½ lb (1.1 kg) redcurrants. The result is a clear jelly of the most delicious flavour and ravishing, clear violet colour.

Bramble Jelly

'. . . the best blackberries are not on the hills, but in the narrow sheltered hill valleys where they hang down over the water, or sweep across the stone-footed dykes, and these blackberries have a richness unknown in the Midlands . . . Ripe blackberries are sometimes a full inch across . . . and simply full of juice, probably on account of the wet land, or from the small water-courses near which they grow best . . . The country people themselves make delicious puddings, jams, wines and jellies from the blackberries and it is to be wished that some of the modern canning and preserving methods could do something more for this delicious fruit.'
Dorothy Hartley THE COUNTRYMAN'S ENGLAND 1935

Pick the blackberries on a dry day. Take a hooked walking stick with you to help pull towards you all those extra fine blackberries that are just out of reach. Also wear wellington boots and trousers. Pick a small proportion of less ripe berries to help the jelly to set. Take them home, pick them over and start cooking them at once.

Put the berries in a deep pan and add ¼ pint (150 ml) water to start them off. Stand the pan in a large pan of water, a sort of deep bain-marie, and put it over a low heat. Leave it for a couple of hours until the juice runs out of the blackberries. Then strain the blackberries through a jelly bag or a cloth. The classic method is to tie the cloth to four legs of a chair turned upside down and placed on top of another chair, and to put a bowl under the cloth on the upturned chair seat. Let the juice drip through gently for some hours, or overnight. Don't squeeze it, or your jelly will not be crystal clear.

Measure the juice and allow 1 lb (450 g) sugar to every 1 pint (550 ml) juice. Put both into a preserving pan, dissolve the sugar by stirring with a wooden spoon over a low heat, then turn up the heat and boil rapidly until setting point is reached. Test a little on a cold saucer every few minutes; when it has cooled it should be stiff enough to wrinkle and stay put. Skim at this point, not before, removing all the froth. Pour into clean, heated jars and cover with waxed paper discs. Allow to cool before covering the pots.

Scales in the kitchen at Great Dixter, East Sussex

copper preserving pan

Lemon Curd

Makes about 1 lb (450 g)

3 oz (75 g) butter

2 lemons

8 oz (225 g) sugar

2 eggs

Heat the butter together with the thinly pared rind of 1 lemon in the top of a double-boiler over hot water. When it has melted, stir in the sugar and the strained juice of 2 lemons and heat gently, stirring until the sugar has dissolved. Remove from the hot water.

Beat the eggs in a bowl, gradually whisk in the butter, sugar and lemon juice mixture and then strain into the top of the double-boiler. Stir over a moderate heat until the mixture thickens to a cream. Pour into a clean heated jar, and allow to cool before eating. Spread it on bread and butter, or use it instead of jam to fill tartlets.

Raspberry Jam

'RASPBERRY JAM
Put the berries and an equal weight of sugar together, on a dish, in the sun till hot, then tilt into a pan, bring to the boil, and cook rapidly 3 minutes; pot while hot and close down.'
Dorothy Hartley FOOD IN ENGLAND 1954

Makes about 5 lb (2.2 kg)

3 lb (1.3 kg) raspberries

3 lb (1.3 kg) sugar

¼ pint (150 ml) redcurrant juice

Put the raspberries into the preserving pan, set on a gentle heat and bring slowly to the boil. Meanwhile warm the sugar in a low oven. Boil the fruit for 2–3 minutes, then add the redcurrant juice and the sugar. Stir over a gentle heat until the sugar has dissolved, then bring to the boil. Boil until setting point is reached (see recipe for bramble jelly, page 151). Remove from the heat, skim and pour into heated jars. Cover with waxed paper discs then leave until cold before covering the jars.

Seville Orange Marmalade

One of the lovely things about Seville in winter is that the streets are lined with orange trees covered with glowing Seville oranges. This is a recipe given to me by an English friend who lives in Spain and grows her own Sevilles. She lets the peel soak for at least 2 days after its first boiling. Use oranges that look nice and fresh, when they start to shrivel the peel gets tough.

Makes 6–6½ lb (2.6–2.9 kg)

3 lb (1.3 kg) Seville oranges

4 lb (1.8 kg) lump sugar

Wash the oranges, cut them in half across and put them in a large pan with 3 pints (1.7 litres) water. Simmer, covered, for 2 hours, bringing the water back to its original level as it boils away. Allow to soak overnight. Bring back to the boil, boil for 1 hour and allow to cool.

Remove the orange halves and take out all the pips, putting them back into the liquid in the pan. Give liquid and pips one last boil and then sieve, working the pips against the sieve with a wooden spoon to get out all the lovely pulp and as much pectin as possible. Warm the sugar, slice the orange halves thinly and cut the slices across into shortish lengths.

Add the sliced peel to the liquid and heat. Tip in the lump sugar and stir over a low heat until it is dissolved. Then turn up the heat and boil until setting point is reached, 220°F (105°C) on a sugar thermometer.

Skim off any scum, allow to cool a little and pour into clean heated jars. Cover with waxed paper discs and cellophane.

'THE ROYAL SANDWICH
This was made with new bread spread with fresh dairy butter, covered with slices of home-cured ham, generously spread with orange marmalade, and topped with more buttered bread.'
Mrs Arthur Webb FARMHOUSE COOKERY c. 1930

A Pennine farmhouse in the shelter of the Worth Valley, West Yorkshire

Light Brandy Sauce

When you put this iced sauce on to the hot Christmas pudding on a hot plate, it melts a little to a delicate foam, and gives a good refreshing shock of hot and cold.

Serves 6

2 egg yolks

2 tbsp granulated sugar

5–6 tbsp brandy

8 fl oz (225 ml) whipping cream, chilled, or ¼ pint (150 ml) double cream and 3 tbsp iced water

1 tbsp icing sugar

½ tbsp vanilla sugar (see below)

Put the egg yolks and granulated sugar in a bowl which fits over a saucepan. Half-fill the saucepan with water and bring to just below boiling point. Whisk the egg yolks and sugar together away from the heat until they are thick, creamy and pale. Put the bowl over the hot water, keeping it always just below boiling point, and pour in the brandy. Whisk continuously until the mixture is thick and light; this takes a while, but will happen eventually.

Pour the boiling water out of the saucepan, half-fill it with cold water and put the bowl back; keep whisking the mixture until it is cool (the contact between the saucepan and the bowl will prevent the latter from cracking).

Put the whipping cream into a large cold bowl and whisk by hand with a balloon whisk or hand beater until it starts to lighten and thicken. Add the icing sugar and vanilla sugar and whisk to a light, but thick, fine foam. Don't overbeat or you will have butter. Fold the brandy mixture into the cream.

Transfer it to a china dish and keep in the ice-making compartment of the refrigerator, or in the freezer until you need it. The brandy will prevent the sauce from freezing too hard.

TO MAKE VANILLA SUGAR
Immerse a vanilla pod in a jar of caster or granulated sugar for at least a week to give it time to pick up the vanilla flavour. It will then keep happily for months. Refill the jar with fresh sugar as you use it up.

Custard

Makes about 1¼ pints (700 ml)

½ vanilla pod

1 pint (550 ml) milk

4 egg yolks

4 oz (100 g) sugar

Split the ½ vanilla pod and put it into a saucepan with the milk. Heat slowly but don't boil. Meanwhile whisk the egg yolks and sugar together until they are pale and creamy. Pour the very hot milk on to the egg and sugar mixture in a slow stream, whisking it in. Return to the pan and place the pan on a heat diffuser or over a very low heat and cook very gently, stirring all the time. The froth will disappear and as the custard starts to thicken so will any large bubbles round the edge.

Remove from the heat when the mixture starts to coat the back of the wooden spoon and strain at once into a bowl. You must never boil custard of this sort as the eggs will curdle instantly, but if a few little lumps form they will disappear when the custard is strained. Serve hot or cold in a pretty jug. Delicious with apple pie (page 116) or greengage crumble (page 115).

155

Bibliography

Acetaria, a Discourse of Sallets
John Evelyn (B. Tooke, 1699; London: Prospect Books, 1982)
Anglo-Indian and Continental Cookery
Mrs Grace Johnson (R. H. Allen & Co., 1893)
The Art of Cookery: A poem in imitation of Horace
William King (London, 1708)
The Art of Cookery Made Plain and Easy
By a Lady [Hannah Glasse] ('Printed for the Author', 1747;
London: Prospect Books, 1983)
A Book of Food
P. Morton Shand (London: Jonathan Cape, 1927)
A Book of Scents and Dishes
Dorothy Allhusen (London: Williams & Norgate, 1926)
Cantaloup to Cabbage
Mrs Philip Martineau (London: Cobden-Sanderson, 1929)
Caviare to Candy
Mrs Philip Martineau (London: Cobden-Sanderson, 1927)
Charcuterie and French Pork Cookery
Jane Grigson (London: Michael Joseph, 1967)
Choice Recipes
Lady Sarah Lindsay (Bentley, 1883)
The Closet of Sir Kenelm Digby Knight, Opened
Sir Kenelm Digby (London, 1669; London: Philip Lee Warner, 1910)
Come Into the Garden Cook
Constance Spry (London: J. M. Dent & Son, 1942)
The Compleat Confectioner
Hannah Glasse (London, *c.* 1760)
The Constance Spry Cooking Book
Constance Spry and Rosemary Hume (London: J. M. Dent & Son, 1956)
The Cook and Housewives' Manual
Mistress Margaret [Meg] Dods [Christian Isobel Johnstone]
(Edinburgh and London: Oliver & Boyd, 1826)
The Cook's Oracle
Dr Kitchiner (London, 1817)
Cottage Economy
William Cobbett (London: published by the author, 1830)
Culinary and Salad Herbs
Eleanour Sinclair Rohde (London: Country Life, 1940)
Culpeper's Complete Herbal
(Manchester: J. Gleave, 1826)
Edible Gifts
Claire Clifton and Martina Nicolls (London: The Bodley Head, 1982)
English Recipes
Countess Morphy (Great Britain, Kent: Herbert Joseph for Selfridges,
c. 1936)
Farmhouse Cookery
Mrs Arthur Webb (London: George Newnes, *c.* 1930)
Farmhouse Cooking
Mark Norwak and Babs Honey (London: Sphere Books, 1973)
Food for Pleasure
Ruth Lowinsky (London: Hart-Davis, 1950)
Food in England
Dorothy Hartley (London: Macdonald, 1954)
Game Birds
Major Hugh B. C. Pollard (London: Eyre & Spottiswoode, 1929)
A Garden of Herbs
Eleanour Sinclair Rohde (London: The Medici Society, *c.* 1920)
The Gentle Art of Cookery
Mrs C. F. Leyel and Miss Olga Hartley (London: Chatto & Windus,
1925)
Good Food for Children
Ambrose Heath (London: Faber & Faber, 1941)
Good Things in England
Florence White (London: Jonathan Cape, 1932)

Gourmet's Book of Food and Drink
Atherton Fleming (London: John Lane, 1933)
The Gourmet's Companion
Cyril Ray (London: Eyre & Spottiswoode, 1963)
The Great British Cheese Book
Patrick Rance (London: Macmillan, 1982)
*The Housekeeper's Guide; or a Plain and Practical System of Domestic
Cookery*
Esther Hewlett Copley (London: Jackson & Walford, 1834)
Irish Traditional Food
Theodora Fitzgibbon (London: Macmillan, 1983)
Jams and Preserves, Bottled Fruits and Vegetables, Chutneys and Pickles
Mary Woodman (London: W. Foulsham)
Kitchen Ranging – a Book of Dish Cover-y
Pearl Adams (London: Jonathan Cape, 1928)
Lady Sysonby's Cook Book
Ria Sysonby (London: Putnam, 1935)
Lovely Food: A Cookery Notebook
Ruth Lowinsky (London: Nonesuch Press, 1931)
Mastering the Art of French Cooking
Simone Beck, Louise Bertholle, Julia Child (New York: Knopf, 1961)
A Medley of Recipes
Dorothy Allhusen (London: Chapman and Hall, 1936)
Minnie Lady Hindlip's Cookery Book
(London: Thornton Butterworth, 1925)
Modern Cookery for Private Families
Eliza Acton (Longman, Brown, Green and Longmans, 1845)
A Modern Herbal
Mrs M. Grieve; edited Mrs C. F. Leyel (London: Jonathan Cape, 1931)
More Lovely Food
Ruth Lowinsky (London: Nonesuch Press, 1935)
A New System of Domestic Cookery
By a Lady [Mrs Maria Eliza Rundle] (London: John Murray, 1806)
Pot Luck or The British Home Cookery Book
May Byron (London: Hodder and Stoughton, 1914)
The Receipt Book of Elizabeth Raper
(1756–70; London: Nonesuch Press, 1924)
Receipts and Relishes
edited Bernard Darwin (The Naldrett Press for Whitbread & Co., 1950)
Recipes from an Old Farmhouse
Alison Uttley (London: Faber & Faber, 1966)
Round the Table
'The G. C.' (London: Horace Cox, 1873)
The Scottish Cookery Book
Elizabeth Craig (London: André Deutsch, 1956)
The Servants' Hall: A Domestic History of Erddig
Merlin Waterson (London: Routledge & Kegan Paul, 1980)
The Sportsman's Cookery Book
Major Hugh B. C. Pollard (London: Country Life, 1926)
The Tenth Muse
Sir Harry Luke (London: Putnam, 1954)
Terrines, Pâtés and Galantines
(Time Life Books, 1981)
Warne's Model Cookery
edited Mary Jewry (Frederick Warne & Co., late nineteenth century)
Weekend Cookery Book
G. M. Boumphrey (London: The Soncino Press, 1932)
Well-tried Dishes
Mrs Annie Kean (London: The Chelsea Publishing Co., 1924)
*A Woman's Work is Never Done, a History of Housework in the British
Isles 1650–1950*
Caroline Davidson (London: Chatto & Windus, 1982)

Index

Picture Acknowledgments

The author and publisher would like to thank the photographers and
institutions whose pictures appear on the following pages:

Castle Museum, York: 138
Fanny Dubes: 39
Good Plain Cookery by Mary Hooper, 1882: 55, 61, 75, 150
Household Management, *c*.1880: 36, 70, 87
Jacqui Hurst: 28, 42, 44, 49, 111
The Mansell Collection: 43
Museum of English Rural Life, Reading: 16 left, 23, 41, 53, 54, 65, 97, 108,
113 below, 118 left, 131, 143, 152 below
Eric Ravilious/*Country Life Cookery Book* by Ambrose Heath: 9, 32, 51,
88, 104, 124, 141; *Notebook*, Kynoch Press, 1933: 129, 132; *The
Writings of Gilbert White of Selborne*, Nonesuch Press, 1938: 1, 155

James Ravilious – The Beaford Archive: 2, 8, 11 above, 13, 24, 27, 30, 35,
40, 47, 50, 55, 58, 62 below, 64, 67, 73, 76, 80, 83, 84, 85, 89, 90 above, 94,
99, 100, 105, 107, 109, 110, 113 above, 117, 125, 126, 127, 130, 133, 134,
139, 140, 147, 149, endpapers
The Royal Horticultural Society, Lindley Library/*The Illustrated
Dictionary of Gardening* by G. Nicholson, 1887: 56, 109, 118 right, 119,
120; *The Vegetable Garden* by W. Robinson, 1905: 11 below, 12, 16
right, 19, 20, 21, 60, 62 above, 71, 91, 93, 95, 96, 101, 102, 103, 144
Pamla Toler: 22, 52, 78 above, 122 above, 145, 152 above
Charlie Waite: 33
Simon Warner: 14, 37, 92, 116, 137, 154

The author and publisher are particularly grateful to James Ravilious for
his unstinting help in supplying his photographs.